Alan Hargrave was born in a terraced house in the middle of Leeds – an area now buried under university and inner-city motorway. He trained as a chemical engineer before working for ten years with the Anglican Church in South America – first on a development project with indigenous people in northern Argentina, then planting churches in Bolivia. He returned to the UK in 1987 to train for the ordained ministry. In 1994 he became the first vicar of Holy Cross, a new parish on a council estate on the edge of Cambridge. In 2004 he became Canon Missioner of Ely Cathedral. In 2001 he published *An Almighty Passion*, a book illustrating the great doctrines of God with stories from ordinary life. He is passionate about mission, unity, justice, cricket, golf, narrowboats, his four children – one of whom tragically died of cancer – his grandchildren, his wife Annie and, of course, the Almighty.

Living Well

Finding a 'Rule of Life'
to revitalize and sustain us

Alan Hargrave

Canon Missioner, El
Cathedral

First published in Great Britain in 2010

Society for Promoting Christian Knowledge
36 Causton Street
London SW1P 4ST
www.spckpublishing.co.uk

The author and publisher have made every effort to ensure that the external website
and email addresses included in this book are correct and up to date at the time
of going to press. The author and publisher are not responsible for the content,
quality or continuing accessibility of the sites.

Unless otherwise noted, Scripture quotations are the author's own translation.

The extract from the Authorized Version of the Bible (The King James Bible),
the rights in which are vested in the Crown, is reproduced by permission
of the Crown's Patentee, Cambridge University Press.

Material taken from *Common Worship: Services and Prayers* is
© Archbishops Council 2000. Used by permission.

British Library Cataloguing-in-Publication Data
A catalogue record for this book is available from the British Library

ISBN 978–0–281–06236–2

Typeset by Graphicraft Ltd, Hong Kong
First printed in Great Britain by J F Print Ltd, Sparkford
Subsequently digitally printed in Great Britain

For two friends who loved me:

Frank Gouthwaite, challenging, infuriating and deeply committed, who, with Peggy, dedicated his life to service among the poor in Brazil.

Tom Corkill who, with Liz, gave us a home when we needed one and loved me enough to tell me my faults, face to face.

And for my grandchildren, Joshua, Lucia, Ximena and the others I hope will join them. May you find the way and may it bring you life.

Contents

Acknowledgements   ix
Preface   xi
Introduction   xiii

1 A personal journey   1
  Taizé   1
  South America   2
  Iona   4
  The Desert Fathers   5
  Turvey Abbey   6
  Cursillo   8
  Newer communities   11
  Etheldreda   12
  Benedict   16

2 Listen   19
  Listening to God in prayer   20
  Sacred space   24
  Listening to God through the Bible   27
  Praying the Psalms   33
  Listening to others   36
  Silence   42
  Speaking   46
  Obedience   51

Contents

3 Stability   59
   Faithfulness   64

4 Work   69
   Work/work balance   71
   Humility   75
   Simplicity   77
   Hospitality   84
   Rest and recreation   88
   Inability to work   91

5 Transformation   97
   A big vision   102
   Interruptions   105

6 Beginning   111

Postscript   115
Appendix 1 The Community of St Etheldreda,
           Ely Cathedral   117
Appendix 2 Ely Cursillo Rule of Life   119
Appendix 3 Summary of the Rule of the Northumbria
           Community   122
Appendix 4 The Rule of the Iona Community   124
Appendix 5 Moot Rhythm of Life   127
Notes   129

Acknowledgements

Apart from those mentioned in the text I am grateful to all those friends, colleagues and family members who have in turn supported, inspired, challenged and infuriated me – especially those who have stood by me over many years. I mention, in particular, my mum and dad and Annie, who has shared the journey with me for most of my life.

In the context of this book I am particularly grateful to those with whom we have shared in communal living, some of whom lived with us at great personal cost.

I am grateful to my colleagues, past and present, including my cathedral colleagues, for putting up with my outspokenness, endless new initiatives and inappropriate dress code.

Finally I am grateful for those who introduced me to the Rule of Benedict, in particular the Community of Turvey Abbey and Peter Sills, and those who have tried to live it out with me, including the small, nascent Community of St Etheldreda.

Note

Some people's names haves been changed, but the situations described are real.

We propose, therefore, to establish a school of the Lord's service, and in setting it up we hope we shall lay down nothing that is harsh or hard to bear . . . Do not then be overcome with terror and run away from the way of salvation, for its beginning must needs be difficult.   *Rule of Benedict*

If this rule were ever to be regarded as an end in itself and to exempt us from ever more seeking to discover God's design, the love of Christ and the light of the Holy Spirit, we would be imposing on ourselves a useless burden; it would have been better never to have written it.   *Rule of Taizé*

The renewal of the church will come from a new type of monasticism which only has in common with the old an uncompromising allegiance to the sermon on the mount. It is high time that men and women banded together to do this.[1]

Dietrich Bonhoeffer

Never doubt that a small group of thoughtful, committed people can change the world. Indeed, it is the only thing that ever has.

Margaret Mead

Change one thing.   *Boots advert*

Preface

In the course of my work I meet a lot of people, typically in their 50s, who are frustrated, disappointed, exhausted, cynical, embittered even. These are often people who, thirty years ago, were committed, enthusiastic and ready to change the world. Yet now the light has gone out of their eyes and they are hanging in for a pension – or have taken one early. At the other end of the scale I look at those in their 20s and 30s, juggling the competing demands of work, ambition, finances, mortgage, relationships with partners and bringing up kids. For such people church can often be bad news rather than good news, since, in a tight schedule where there is no slack, it demands yet more of our time to attend meetings and sit on committees.

How can these young people avoid becoming like the generation above them? And how can those for whom 'the light has gone out of their eyes' re-capture the sparkle? What way of life, what 'rule', will revitalize and sustain us, not just for the big event or the special occasion, which we can all rise to, but for 20, 30, 50 years of joyful service and well-lived life to come?

The purpose of this book is to help us think through the pattern of our living in order to find a 'Rule' that will not just sustain us, but also allow us to look beyond ourselves, to make a difference and to have a life ourselves. By 'Rule' I am not referring to a set of rules and regulations. I mean, rather, a way of living, a rhythm or pattern of life, that determines the shape of our lives. It is not so much a list of 'dos' and 'don'ts' as about the fundamental principles by which we, as individuals and as communities, choose to live. In order to help us find a life-giving pattern of living for ourselves, I have included some exercises and resources which you might like to think about on your own or, preferably, together with others.

Fortunately, we are not starting from scratch, because, over the centuries, particularly (but not exclusively) in the monastic tradition, people have developed 'Rules of Life', to help us live well. (Some relatively modern rules are included in the Appendices.) Living under such rules is not a guarantee of success. Some have been hurt by the imposition of 'Rules' that are harsh or even abusive. A friend of ours, who was a nun for many years, refers to herself as 'in permanent recovery from obedience'. Neither is this book a commentary on Benedict's or any other Rule. There are many excellent scholars, such as Esther de Waal, who already offer this.[1] It is rather a journey to find a set of principles which are both flexible and adaptable, a personal 'Rule of Life' as well as a way of living well with others, of becoming a life-giver, so that, God willing, the light in our eyes might continue to shine, well into old age. Leonardo Boff reminds us, as we embark on this journey, that 'The deposit of faith is not a stagnant cistern. It is a spring of Living Water.'[2]

These were lofty goals, appealing to our naive, youthful idealism. But, others were doing it too: Scargill House, Lee Abbey,
the Fisherfolk.[3] Well, if *they* could do it then why not *us*? Surely
this was how to live if we wanted to take discipleship seriously
and be effective in serving others?

Yet the 'socket incident' made us realize that, in order to live
together, we needed some ground rules. How did we make
decisions? How could we accommodate individual personality
and preference? What were our different responsibilities? What
was to be the basic pattern of our life together? Up until now
we had concentrated on the practicalities, hoping that if we
sorted the electrics, painted the rooms, put a heater in the
bathroom and got rid of the mice that lived off Frank's Weetabix,
all would be well. Now we needed to focus on the really essential
things: our relationships; how we shared and prayed together;
how we could live together well; whether we could live together
at all.

And with the need for some common ground rules came the
realization that each of us already had his or her own particular rules. In-built. Unquestioned. Completely normative for each
one of us, but often alien to everyone else. Frank objected to
me throwing my coat on the sofa when I came in instead of
hanging it up. When I replied: 'Well, what about your gloves
which you throw on the floor behind the door when *you* come
in, eh?' he told me that that was where his gloves belonged,
whereas I'd just thrown my coat on the sofa out of laziness.
Anyone who has got married or lived with others for any length
of time knows all about this. Loving one another, being committed to an ideal – these things just aren't enough on their
own. It is a strange paradox. In order to discover the freedom
to live together well and the grace to achieve our common
purpose, we need some clear boundaries and agreed ways of
doing things that will liberate us from being bogged down by

the petty and unimportant, in order to reach a higher goal. And this involves two things that seem sharply counter-cultural in our day – agreed rules and self-discipline.

Within a couple of years Frank had given up a promising academic career, and Peggy her teaching, and they were off to do agricultural development in a poor, rural area of Brazil. A couple of years after that, Annie and I, after living communally with two other friends and their children, would follow them to South America. Over the next thirty plus years our experience of living and working with others would determine how well we were, or were not, able to be part of God's mission. What 'Rule' would enable us to do this well? What Rule would serve us well as individuals, to live full, balanced lives? What Rule would enable us to live creatively and well with others? What Rule would enable the communities of which we were a part to fulfil their vocations effectively?

And more importantly still, what Rule will enable me to live and work well with my colleagues in the Cathedral now? What principles do we need in order to allow our different gifts to flourish and our different ways of doing things to be complementary, rather than conflicting? And what can I do so that my colleagues are not driven to despair by my need to express opinions at length on every subject, by my endless suggestions for new initiatives, my bottomless pit of anecdotes, my outspoken directness, by the apparent ease with which I would happily overturn a thousand years of tradition, and by my coloured shoelaces, baggy jumpers and lack of familiarity with the ironing board?

What 'Rule' do you live by?

Table 1 (overleaf) can be downloaded from <www.elycathedral. org/worship/spirituality> – Rule of Life Questionnaire. Some examples are included here to help you think about filling it in.

Table 1 Rule of Life questionnaire

What do you actually do every day, week, month, year to sustain and grow . . .	Every day	Every week	Every month	Every year
1 Your relationships with loved ones, family and close friends?	Text my wife.	Do a bit of phoning and Facebooking to catch up.	See children/ grandchildren.	Big family get-together.
2 Your relationships with work colleagues?	Emails!	Weekly staff meetings. Pop in to Centre.		Annual staff outing. Staff reviews.
3 Your relationships with neighbours and community?		Mmmm. I think I have neglected this.	Visit Silvia. Chat to local 'winos'.	
4 Your relationship with the wider world?	Follow news on BBC, Al Jazeera and other websites.		Pray for our link churches in Hackney and Zanzibar.	Write to our friends in Uganda. Review giving.
5 Your spiritual life/ relationship with God/your own soul?	Say Daily Office with others.		See Spiritual Director every 3 months.	Silent retreat. Greenbelt?
6 Your own personal health and well-being?	I'm not very good at this . . . Flop in front of cricket on TV.	Play golf. Cycle.	Bloke-ish 3-day golfing extravaganza every 4 months	

- Is there anything that surprises you about what you've written? Are there particular 'gaps' you need to work on?
- Are there special places associated with any of the above?
- What one thing would you like to change in order to get a better balance in your life?
- In one sentence, what is your personal 'Rule of Life'?
- Do you have a 'Rule' you share with others – partner/colleagues/ friendship group/Church/community?
- Is there anyone you feel accountable to for how you live your life?

1

A personal journey

Dear God . . . Across the difficult terrain of our existence we have attempted to build a highway and in so doing have lost our footpath. God lead us to our footpath. God lead us where in simplicity we may move at the speed of natural creatures and feel the earth's love beneath our feet . . . Nothing can be loved at speed. God lead us to the slow path; to the joyous insights of the pilgrim; another way of knowing: another way of being.[1]

Taizé

In 1972, we planned, for our summer holidays, to hitch-hike around France. At a party in Birmingham, just before we left, someone mentioned Taizé. 'You ought to go there. It's amazing. And it's not far from where you are heading.' We'd never heard of it but, after some wrong directions and, finally, hitching a lift from a very hippy-looking VW Kombi, we made it. Coming from an evangelical, charismatic church, it was like nothing we'd ever experienced before; not at all what we were used to and certainly not what we had come to think of as 'sound'. No one was telling us how to be saved. Yet thousands of young people from all over Europe, from many different church traditions and none, were just turning up, like us, without having booked in. Eating aubergine stew, baring our souls to strangers and discovering, within the beauty of the simple, repetitive

1

worship, transcendence, mystery, paradox and the Holy Spirit flowing among us in a way we could not deny, understand or tie down to a formula.

And something else. Something about the quality of the shared life of the brothers. About the contrast between those thousands of unkempt young people from across Europe and the clean, clear, deeply attractive simplicity of the common life of the Taizé Community. It reminded me of words from Psalm 19:

> The precepts of the LORD are right, rejoicing the heart:
> The commands of the LORD are radiant, giving light to
> the eyes.
> The fear of the LORD is clean, enduring for ever: The
> ordinances of the LORD are true and righteous
> altogether.
> More to be desired are they than gold, even much fine
> gold; Sweeter also than honey and the drippings of the
> honeycomb.[2]

There was pure gold here, very sweet and desirable. This was our first contact with a monastic community. What was it about the monks, and the way they lived together, ecumenically, that was so obviously resulting in a most amazing work of God? For the first time, our clear, certain faith began to open itself to the possibility that there might just be other ways of seeing things. Could it be the case that, in some areas at least, we might, just possibly, be wrong?

South America

After another wonderful and painful experience of living communally with our friends Jim and Lorrie, this time involving children, we headed off to South America. Living in the remote Chaco area of northern Argentina, we soon discovered that 'choice' was something most people around the world didn't have much of. Shopping was basic. The choice of bread was – if they had any – you bought it, before they ran out. Cold meat? A powerful garlic salami – or nothing. Fresh meat? 'He's not slaughtering the pig until tomorrow.' And accommodation, too. We lived in a prefab made of asbestos sheets. The supporting timbers were almost completely devoured by termites. The house moved in the wind and was held up by a brick shed on one side and a brick 'lean to' on the other. We didn't have any choice about where we lived or who we lived with. In fact, for our first three years we lived in a traditional missionary compound, closely bound together with an Argentine educationalist, two nurses, from Australia and Yorkshire, and an indigenous family. In some ways it made life much simpler – but in others more difficult. We were all very different. When someone came from England with Cadbury's chocolate, we ate all ours immediately. Deferred gratification did not form part of our family 'rule'. Mary and Jean, on the other hand, ate one square each and then put the rest back in the fridge, to be opened and eaten sparingly, on special occasions, over the next 18 months.

Our choice was not to find a place we liked, among people we thought we might get on with. We were not able to move house or change jobs. Our choice was to make it work, however difficult we found the people we were with. This is an important discipline. Very often we find it easier to blame others than to do the painful work of removing the plank in our own eye,[3] which will, ultimately, enable us to see God and each other with greater love and compassion.

The contrast with our Western living, where choice seems never ending, could not have been more stark. After three years we returned home on leave, via Miami, where we spent the night in a motel. Wandering into the local 'grocery store', which turned out to be the biggest hypermarket we'd ever seen, we stood transfixed in front of the huge array of products, unable to choose between 30 different varieties of cold meat and 40 different types of bread. Choice offers us the possibility of something new, something different, a way of escape. Yet so many of our choices are trivial, driven more by aggressive marketing rather than by our needs. They can so easily fool us into thinking that happiness and fulfilment dwell at the end of a series of correct purchases, rather than through living well, wherever we happen to find ourselves.

Another stark contrast came in decision-making. Argentines, for the most part, operate in a 'macho' culture, where the charismatic leader makes the decisions and inspires or directs others to follow. The indigenous people had quite a different method of deciding. They would sit and talk for hours, days or weeks even, until everyone had had their say. The leader would then reflect back to the community the decision he believed they had made, after he felt a consensus had been reached. That is not to say that everyone held the same opinion, but that everyone came to a point where they could support the decision that was being taken. Thus when it came to forming a company to sell handicrafts and produce from the cooperative farm, the leader of the 400-strong owner-workforce informed us that there was one thing they would not do under any circumstances, and that was to vote. 'Why not?' we asked. 'Once we vote', he said, 'we set one group against another and create divisions. It is better for us to decide all together.' This concept of consensus, though easy to idealize and difficult in practice, is nevertheless at the heart of gospel living.[4]

Iona

In 1993 I went on retreat to Iona. I had come across the Iona Community over a period of years through their music and drama, through their work with young people from inner-city Glasgow, as well as their stand for justice and peace. Their liturgy seemed to speak in everyday language and capture creatively what they proclaimed and lived, reflecting the interweaving of the physical and spiritual which is so evident in Celtic spirituality. Having been inspired by my time there, I decided to join the Iona Community. However, that was before I had read their 'Rule'.[5] I agreed with it wholeheartedly. But I knew I couldn't keep it. It would have committed me to a daily discipline of prayer and Bible reading that was beyond my capability. I had tried for years to keep up my daily pattern of Bible reading and prayer, but had consistently failed, managing only two or three days a week, at best. Not only that, but it never seemed to give me the promised sense of God's presence, of God speaking to me, which people talked about. Maybe there was something wrong with me, with my commitment? Whatever it was, recognizing my own limitations became an important part of discovering what 'Rule' might – and might not – work for me. A rule clearly needs to challenge and stretch us. Yet if it constantly leaves us despairing and defeated, it does not take us forward in our spiritual journey.

The Desert Fathers

About that time I picked up a copy of *The Wisdom of the Desert*.[6] It contains stories of the Desert Fathers, the first Christian hermits who lived in the deserts of Egypt and the Middle East. These stories describe some of the extraordinary events of their lives. For a modern Western reader the stories are somewhat enigmatic. The way the monks behave, the advice they give, how they relate to one another, their attitude to women, how they relate to visitors and their spiritual experience often appear surprising, if not shocking, to us. Yet their pithy, unsentimental wisdom has a strange attraction. They battle demons and argue with the devil. Their life is harsh and their words are blunt. They perform extraordinary miracles and engage in remarkable acts of self-denial. They do not suffer fools gladly but are capable of great compassion and generosity. Their rule is not written down in any logical formula: it is contained within the stories.

Maybe that's why I find them so attractive? For me, and perhaps for many people, stories provide a better way towards understanding than abstract concepts. In our everyday lives we hear someone relate the story of a difficult rail journey, or of a spell in hospital, and we say: 'Exactly the same thing happened to me!' We identify with their experience.

In many ways this is how we proclaim our faith liturgically. As we re-enact the last supper in our communion services, the story of Jesus and his disciples sharing the Passover meal becomes *our* story. We are re-enacting the events of that first Easter. We become the characters in the story. *We* are the disciples, gathered around the table with Jesus at the centre. *We* share his body broken, his blood poured out for us. *We* celebrate his resurrection. *We* go out to proclaim the Good News. So too, as we read these strange stories from the desert, we are caught up in them as they reflect, often in unexpected ways, the struggles, temptations and experience of our own spiritual journey. Hence this book is not just about 'Rules', which can seem dry and dull. It is also about stories, which, for many of us, make the abstract concrete and bring words to life.

Turvey Abbey

During the 1990s I began to take a regular retreat, first at St Mary's, Wantage, and then at Turvey Abbey, a Roman Catholic Benedictine community of women and men. In these two places I discovered silence, and found I was poor at it. I discovered that I was not good company for myself, and God didn't seem to provide very good company either. I found it hard to concentrate, with all manner of things filling my mind. I could see the theory, that here was an opportunity to listen to God, unmediated, on my own. But in practice, for the most part, it seemed like a barren, empty place. A place full of my own worries and struggles but without much sense of God's presence, whatever that might mean.

The one place where I found a sense of silence and an ability to listen was in the chapel, particularly in the 'Offices', the daily worship services, which somehow carried me even when I was unable to join in. It was as though there existed, in that place, a sense of prayerfulness, stillness, receptiveness, presence, which I didn't create, but which existed in the community and which I was invited to become a part of, for a short while. Furthermore, to my surprise, these nuns (it was mostly the nuns I had contact with) did not match the rather plain, pious, dour caricature I had in my mind. These were lively, creative women with a bit of spark; women who made things of great beauty, spoke with passion, enjoyed a laugh and seemed earthed in everyday life.

What was so striking about the BBC TV series *The Monastery*, where five ordinary blokes were invited to live with the monks of Worth Abbey for six weeks, was that the people you might choose as mates, the ones you'd really want to have a jar with down the pub, were not the men off the street. They were, rather, the Worth Abbey monks themselves. Far from the monastery separating people from real life, the monks seemed to be very attuned to ordinary life; attractive people, full of spark.

Like Turvey, Worth Abbey is also a Benedictine house. Yet each community has developed its own particularity and character, as well as its own gifts. The community at Ditchingham, for example, has a rule that says: 'The sisters shall keep silence,

except at tea-time when they shall be merry and bright' –
presumably whether they feel like it or not!

Here is an important issue for us to consider. On the one
hand, too much choice can be a snare for us. On the other, we
need to discover what is helpful for us, what fits in with
our personal inner rhythms; our own characters and gifts. The
challenge is to keep these things in *balance*, a concept to which
we shall return.

Cursillo

In the mid 1990s I was looking for a discipleship course that
would work well with people who were not the articulate
middle-classes. I looked at Alpha, but the smart, professional-
looking people on the video seemed to me a million miles from
the council estate community in which I was working. We tried
one or two other courses with mixed success. Then someone
invited me on a Cursillo[7] weekend. I wasn't really sure what I
was letting myself in for, which was just as well or I would never
have gone. The weekend took us, experientially, from Maundy
Thursday through to Easter Sunday. It was exhausting, annoy-
ing and full of surprises. My biggest surprise was that, despite
my reservations about some of the content and the feeling that
I'd sometimes been manipulated, I came away richly blessed,
having been touched by God in a quite remarkable way.

The really great thing about it was the way it was led by lay
people from all sorts of backgrounds. People who were not
particularly confident or articulate found a voice and a place
where their contribution could be heard, recognized, valued
and used. A number of people from our estate went on it and
found it life-changing. It achieved in a weekend what I had
failed to achieve in several years of discipleship groups. And
it was not just a 'three-day wonder', because it also provided an

ongoing community to belong to, opportunities for service and a simple 'Rule' for living.[8]

Perhaps what I valued more than anything else was that Cursillo was a place where I could be really open and honest. Sadly, that has by no means always been my experience of church. I attended, recently, a seminar at Greenbelt where a number of people spoke about why they had left the Church.[9] None of them said it was because they didn't believe in God any more. Most of them spoke of having concerns about areas of belief or practice, or about difficult issues they were wrestling with in their own lives. However, when they tried to discuss these at church they generally found they were corrected, given simplistic answers or prayed for, that they might 'get back on track'. What they wanted was a place where they could engage with others openly and honestly. What they found was a door closed to discussion. Hence, after long struggles, they left their churches, though most of them have continued to belong to small 'homegroups' where they feel they can be both honest and accepted.

I remember myself playing golf with a clergyman I didn't know very well, a few months after our son had died. He asked me about Tom and about myself. I explained that I sometimes wondered if God existed at all and talked to him about how hard it was to share this with my parishioners, who looked to me for spiritual leadership. 'Oh,' he said gravely, 'it's not good to be too honest with people.' But what have we to fear from being honest and open? When I have been honest about my own doubts and fears, people suddenly have begun to talk about their own. 'We didn't realize clergy had doubts,' they say. 'It's so good to know that you've struggled with that as well.'

The surprising thing about openness and honesty is that it breeds openness and honesty. I recall observing an unemployed, disabled woman from my parish speaking with a lawyer and a banker at a Cursillo weekend. Her honesty about her own drink problem and her daughter's drug addiction broke through their well-built defences and enabled them to speak openly about the pain and difficulties in their own lives. And this is not easy for us, since, despite what it says on the church 'tin', many, including myself, instead of understanding and acceptance, have experienced rejection and exclusion. If we are seriously seeking the truth about God and about ourselves, what have we to fear from honesty and openness? – providing, of course, we ourselves are open to challenge and to change.

This also ties in with the results of an internet survey devised by John Drane.[10] He asked people to put a set of words into one of two columns marked 'Spirituality' and 'Religion'. They then had to put the words 'yes' or 'no' in each column. The results were remarkably uniform. Table 2 shows some of the words.

Table 2

Spirituality	Religion
Free	Rigid
Development	Static
Open	Closed
Interior	External
Experience	Reason
Searching	Dogmatic
Questions	Answers
Journey	Arrived
Relationship	Structures
Action	Words
Yes	No

Exercise

Repeat the above exercise yourself, as it relates to your own church. Ask other church members to do it. Then ask some people who rarely come to church to fill in the survey. Have a discussion, perhaps at the church council, about the results, about what words you'd *like* to describe your church or group, and about what you need to change so that they do.

Newer communities

It is perhaps surprising to find each year at Greenbelt, a Christian Arts Festival held at Cheltenham Racecourse and attracting many thousands of young people, several speakers from religious communities. And, as well as that, a growing interest among young people in embracing a 'Rule of Life' to guide them through a rapidly changing world. One such community is 'Moot', a group of young Christians based in London who agree to live by a common 'Rhythm'.[11] More established is the 'Northumbria Community'. They have a rule that essentially consists of just two, very challenging, words: Availability and Vulnerability.[12]

It is not necessary to become a nun or a monk in order to live by a rule. Since the series *The Monastery* was broadcast, Worth Abbey has around 6,000 lay people coming on retreat each year. Thousands of ordinary people are Franciscan Tertiaries, Benedictine Oblates or members of other 'lay' communities. Many more are learning from those in religious communities how to discover life through long-established spiritual disciplines.

Exercise

1 Take some time to write about your own spiritual journey. What have been the major influences on your life? What has helped you follow more closely in the way of Christ? What have been the major influences in helping you find a 'rule to live by'?

2 What communities are you a part of? How do they influence the way you live? Are the Christian communities you are a part of places where you feel as if you are walking together with others by a common rule or rhythm? Are they places where you can be completely open and honest?

3 What other communities might you explore as a means of thinking more seriously about a 'Rule of Life'? Are there other people who might join you in this venture?

Etheldreda

Some years ago one of our bishops suggested I might work in a cathedral. 'I don't think so,' I replied. 'Cathedrals are hotbeds of privilege, elitism and establishment – definitely not for me!' Three years later a different bishop pointed me to a job going at Ely Cathedral. I made a similar remark. He suggested that I at least get the job description and have a look. As I read through it, I was amazed. 'This is my dream job,' I thought. I was even more astonished when, after the interviews, I was appointed. Only then did I begin to see cathedrals in a new light.

Becoming part of the Cathedral community was not easy for me, and I dare say not easy for the Cathedral community either. My dress code was not quite up to muster for a kick-off. I had no idea how to swing a thurible or wear a cope. I had never heard of the 'Howells' Responses', and I didn't know the difference between an acolyte and an aconite. And I wondered how I had managed to be a vicar for 11 years without ever having produced a single set of Rubrics. It was a steep learning curve, yet one which has brought rich blessing to me, and which, I hope, has not all been one-way. And I began, among other things, to learn about Etheldreda. Indeed, because of Etheldreda and her monastery in Ely, we began to develop a small community, for people connected with the Cathedral and Diocese, seeking to follow a simple rule together, loosely based on the Rule of Benedict.[13]

Etheldreda was a Saxon princess who lived in Exning, near Newmarket. She came from a devout family, and from an early age Etheldreda felt called to the religious life. However, her father, King Anna, was more concerned with strengthening his kingdom, so she was married to Tonbert, King of Fenmen, who, for a wedding present, gave her the Isle of Ely, a stretch of high ground that rose above the fenland marshes between Ely and Wisbech. Tonbert soon died, but instead of being allowed to pursue her religious vocation, another politically expedient marriage was arranged. This time it was to Egfrid, Prince of Northumbria, the most powerful kingdom in the land. However, Egfrid was still a teenager, so Etheldreda was, for a time, able to live the religious life. She came under the influence of Bishop Wilfrid, an important though not very likeable figure, who was largely responsible for bringing the English Church into line with Rome. He encouraged her in her vocation to the religious life. After his father died, Egfrid became king and wanted to consummate the marriage and produce an heir. Etheldreda's conflicted loyalties to the kingdom and to her religious calling finally came to a head. She left her husband and ran away to Ely. In AD 673 she founded a monastery of men and women, of which she was the Abbess, the head. She was not the only woman in such a position: Hilda, her aunt, was Abbess of a similar mixed monastery in Whitby. It reminds us that women in leadership in the church is not such a recent phenomenon as some of us might like to think.

Six years later, in AD 679, Etheldreda died. Yet such was the quality of her life, and the many 'miracles' associated with her both before and after her death, that pilgrims began to flock to Ely. This was no mean feat, as Ely was surrounded by water and marshland. There were just a few difficult causeways crossing the fen. Access was mainly by river. (The extent of Ely's isolation is clearly shown in that it was the last place where the Saxons, under Hereward the Wake, held out against the Norman conquest.) Many pilgrims travelled via Ely on their way to Walsingham. They came seeking healing, forgiveness and guidance, and to offer thanks to God. Ely became one of the three most important centres of pilgrimage in medieval England.

In many ways Etheldreda was a very human figure, a woman torn by conflicting loyalties, no stranger to mixed motives. A woman who, like many across the world today, struggled under the authority of men. She was a woman pulled in two incompatible directions by her sense of duty and loyalty, both to God and to her Saxon kingdom. She was someone many of us might relate to today.

We know very little about the 'rule' that Etheldreda's community embraced. A small snippet from the *Liber Eliensis*,[14] a twelfth-century manuscript, recently translated into English, tells us: 'They all kept to one and the same rule: outstanding virtue and the maintenance of the house of God with all watchfulness.' To virtue we will return later.

This brief description of the monastic way of life reminds me of a project set by a friend of mine for her Year 7 pupils. Ely Diocese was setting up a new parish to minister to people from a large council estate that had been built since the Second World War, and I was to be the first vicar. Diana asked her class to send me a letter and a drawing, describing what they felt I needed for the new church. The letters all began: 'Dear Vicar Hargrave, What you need for your new church is . . .' There were some intriguing suggestions: 'the Vicar's shed'; 'an ice-cream van'; 'a big TV'. However, the two most popular suggestions by far were 'stained-glass windows' and a 'hostel for homeless people'. These seemed to me to capture something absolutely central about the church's mission. Stained glass – something that takes us beyond ourselves, that gives us a sense of wonder, of transcendence, that lifts us to God. Something that resonates with Etheldreda's 'maintaining the beauty of the house of God'. And the homeless hostel: reaching out to the poor, the needy, the vulnerable, the lost. Perhaps this chimes with 'outstanding virtue' and the call of religious communities to 'hospitality', another theme to which we shall return.

One thing we do know is that Etheldreda lived a hundred years or so after Benedict, whose Rule spread quickly across Europe in the years after his death. We know, too, that Bishop Wilfrid, who was such a formative influence on Etheldreda, was a great advocate of Benedict's Rule. So it is highly likely that her monastery kept the 'Rule of Benedict' from the very beginning. Etheldreda's monastery was destroyed by the Danes in AD 870 but rebuilt by Benedictine monks, for men only, in AD 970. The Saxon abbey was then rebuilt by the Normans, the present day 'cathedral' dating from 1080.

It is to Benedict and his Rule that we must now turn.

Exercise

1 Etheldreda's story is of someone struggling with mixed feelings and divided loyalties. She faced a life that brought her inner conflict. What inner conflicts do you struggle with? What difficult dilemmas do you face? Who might you turn to for help with these?

2 Etheldreda clearly accepted Wilfrid's spiritual authority over her. She confided in him her personal struggles and dilemmas, and looked to him for guidance. Is there anyone whose wisdom and insight you respect, in whom you can confide and share your own personal dilemmas; someone who will be really honest with you, who will keep you grounded and help you think through important decisions?

3 Etheldreda, quite shockingly for her day, broke the mould of convention to become a nun. What current conventions, about the way we live now, hinder your ability to live well and to bring life to others? How might you dare to be different, even if it is not necessarily understood or admired by those around you?[15]

4 If you had to start from scratch and redesign your church, what would be the two most important elements that you would want to include – and why? What priority do these two things have in your church as it is at present? Would it be possible to change those priorities?

5 Etheldreda lived a short but very important life, the fruits of which continue to bring blessing to people today. If you were to die today, what would your legacy be? If you were to live for another ten years, what would you want it to be then?

Benedict

Benedict was born in Italy towards the end of the fifth century, about 70 years after the fall of Rome in AD 410.[16] His world was an uncertain, troubled, dangerous place; the '*Pax Romana*' a distant memory. Benedict came from a well-off family and studied in Rome, but abandoned his studies to live as a hermit. Gradually others gathered around him. Eventually he moved with some of his monks to Monte Cassino, where he remained until his death in AD 547. Benedict wrote a 'Rule' for his community, which draws heavily on the Bible and on previous monastic 'rules'. He rejects both the extreme asceticism of some monastic traditions[17] and also the decadence of others. His Rule contains great wisdom, balance and compassion. Much of the life of the community was based around the Scriptures, which were central both to worship and to personal meditation, study and formation.

Most modern books have a shelf-life of a couple of years at the most. Benedict's Rule has remained a best-seller for 1500 years. It is a measure of its enduring quality that today it is being used not just by monastic communities and lay people in their everyday lives, but even as a guide for those in business. It provides us with a helpful framework as we think about what 'Rule' might help us, and the communities to which we belong, to think about how we should live our lives. It is important to bear in mind that Benedict's Rule, like other rules, is a careful balance of a number of different, often competing, factors. For Benedict there is no single, magic solution that will transform our lives. It holds together in tension a series of disciplines, designed to filter out egocentric preoccupations which often consume so much of our energy; for example, our preoccupation as a society with how we look, our physical shape, what we eat, what clothes we wear, what products we rub or spray on our bodies, how others see us. Instead his Rule is intended to open up a way of life that releases the monks to draw closer to God. Even today, for many who would not count themselves Christians or part of the Church it holds a powerful resonance for authentic living. This is not like a multi-choice exam: 'Answer any three of the ten questions below.' It is a complete package, all of which needs to be kept in careful balance.

Although the rest of this book draws on a number of different 'Rules', it is the Rule of Benedict, far and away the most influential Rule in the Christian Church, that will give this book its basic shape.

Exercise

1 Looking back over the past three months, what areas of your life do you think you have been overly preoccupied with? What areas have been neglected?

2 You may wish to keep a journal, as you read through this book, making a note of those things you believe need greater attention and those that are consuming too much of your energies.

3 Think about some of the key groups you belong to and discuss with them whether you think you have a right balance in the different areas in which you are involved together. What things need to have a higher priority? What things are draining your resources in an unproductive way?

Resources

www.iona.org.uk – information about the Iona Community.

www.northumbriacommunity.org – information about the Northumbria Community.

www.retreats.org.uk – an organization embracing most of the major Christian denominations which provides information about places of retreat in the UK. It publishes a journal in December each year, *Retreats*, a guide to retreat centres and their programmes.

www.Taizé.fr/en – information about the Taizé Community.

www.tssf.org.uk – information about becoming a Franciscan 'tertiary'.

www.turveyabbey.org.uk – see 'Retreats and Courses'.

www.ukcursillo.org – information about the Cursillo movement. 'Cursillo' began in the Roman Catholic Church in Spain and has spread across the world to all major denominations. Cursillo means 'a little course' (in Christianity).

www.worthabbey.org.uk – see 'Open Cloister'.

2

Listen

Listen my son to the instructions of your Master, turn the ear of your heart to the advice of a loving father.[1]

The first word in Benedict's rule is 'listen'.

The first, and perhaps most important, discipline is to listen. How very hard this is, especially for someone like me who is a born talker, who always seems to have something to say on any subject, irrespective of the paucity of my knowledge of it. And indeed Benedict contrasts listening with speaking, which he rarely allows:

> Because of the great importance of keeping silence, permission to speak should be rarely given, even to exemplary disciples.[2]

We need of course to bear in mind that Benedict is writing for monks. Nevertheless, the discipline of listening is one of vital importance to all of us. I know from my own pastoral visiting that what is most appreciated by people is not advice, but having the opportunity to be heard. And this is not some memory exercise in which we can later repeat what was said correctly. It is about taking to heart what is said, as well as what is not said. Or perhaps it is said with hands, eyes and body. Listen 'with the ear of your heart', says Benedict. Allow it to get inside you. Let your heart be thrilled with their joy. Let their pain touch you deeply. Whether we are listening to God or listening to another person, attentiveness, openness and concentration are vital. They do not come naturally to most of us. They are disciplines that need practice. They are disciplines that will change us.

Listening to God through the Scriptures and in worship is central to Benedict's Rule. Indeed, when Benedict is talking about work, this is it. The *real* work of God, the '*Opus Dei*', is not tending the farm, cooking the meals, caring for the sick, welcoming visitors, copying the holy books, counting the money or looking after the buildings – however important those things might be. It is prayer, worship, the sacraments and meditation on the Scriptures.

Listening to God in prayer

For Benedict the essential business of the monastery was the maintenance of the 'Daily Offices'. These were a series of seven services, throughout the day and night, based around the chanting of the Psalms. The whole book of 150 Psalms was said each week. Ely Cathedral maintains this tradition with morning and evening prayer and a Eucharist, said or sung each day (though we usually only have three services a day instead of seven, and we read through the Psalms once a month instead of once a week).

Before coming to Ely I had struggled for years with trying to discipline myself to a daily pattern of prayer, which I was unable to keep. I think part of my problem was unrealistic expectation. Enthusiastic friends asked me: 'What has the Lord been teaching you today?' I felt reluctant to reply that during my recent Bible reading and prayer sessions, I had (a) lost my place on several occasions and been unable to remember what I'd read, (b) found it very boring, (c) spent a lot of time thinking about Leeds United, and (d) fallen asleep. It was only when I began to acknowledge this and had honest conversations with others that I discovered that I was not alone in my experience.

At the interview for the Ely job the Dean asked me how I thought I'd get on with having to attend morning and evening worship every day. I replied that I didn't know but that I'd give it my best shot. The truth was that I was worried about entering a tradition that I was not used to. Yet to my surprise I found it liberating. It was like a home-coming for me. Having a clear pattern of prayer laid out each day freed me from the cult of individualism, from having to invent a pattern for myself. The pattern varies from day to day, and also from time to time, reflecting the seasons of Advent, Christmas, Lent, Easter, etc. What was particularly helpful for me was that I was not doing it alone. There were other people praying with me – seven or eight in the morning and ten to 100 each evening.

A former Bishop of Chester conducted a survey of his clergy to see how good they were at sticking to their daily rhythm of prayer and Bible reading. What he discovered was that those who had an informal 'quiet time' tended to lose the pattern quickly when the chips were down, whereas those who followed a daily 'Office' tended to stick with it even when things were going badly.

What happens each morning as I go through the routine of prayer and reading which forms the daily 'Office'? Mostly, for me at least, nothing happens. There are no bright lights. No ecstatic experiences. No 'feel-good factor'. Very, very occasionally, like Ann Lewin's poem 'Watching for the Kingfisher', there might be a flash of blue and gold. Very, very occasionally! But that is the rare exception rather than the rule. For the most part it is work. '*Opus Dei*.' Deliberately coming into God's presence, not because of what I hope to get out of it, but because turning up to read the Scriptures and pray every day is the right thing to do. And for some reason, for me and I suspect for others, it is easier if there are other people there to do it with. (Though, strangely, I often find myself turning up 20 minutes early, to sit alone in silence.)

Finding others to pray with or creating a pattern for ourselves is not always easy, as I found for most of my life before coming to Ely. Increasingly these days, however, there are great resources on the internet to help us. Many people find that downloading a daily meditation and listening to it on their way to work fits well with a demanding schedule or lengthy commuting. It also helps people feel that they are part of a larger community of worshippers, even if they cannot be physically present with them. Indeed, that is the basis of 'common' prayer, that which we do together rather than as individuals. Many of the newer religious communities, along with the 'lay' members of traditional communities, are not localized. They are dispersed. But modern technology allows us to worship together, albeit while geographically separate.

There is a balance to be struck between what helps me as an individual and how I might form part of a wider, community discipline, that may involve others, sometimes worshipping in ways that are not my personal preference. We also need to be mindful of the warning from Taizé: 'Common prayer does not dispense us from personal prayer.'[3]

Sheila Cassidy tells us: 'Pray as you can; not as you can't.' I think I had been trying to 'pray as I couldn't' for years. However, whatever pattern we decide on, whatever pattern suits our own particular psyche and routine, the fundamental thing is to put ourselves, quite deliberately, in that place where we are regularly available to listen to what God might have to say to us.

Exercise

1 Is your current daily pattern of prayer helpful or do you feel the need to change it?

2 Are you most energized by a time alone or is it more helpful to you to pray with others? Who might you approach to pray with on a regular basis, perhaps once or twice a week at least? What is going on in your vicinity that you might join in with?

3 What is the best time of day for you to pray? Do you do find a clear structure or a more extemporary approach most helpful?

4 Why not have a look at some of the daily devotion material, in book form or on the internet, that you are not currently familiar with?

Resources

These are just some of the very many resources available. You might care also to browse in your local Christian bookshop or talk with others about what they find useful.

Books

Common Worship: Daily Prayer, published by Church House. This is an Anglican compendium of Daily Worship, containing Morning and Evening Prayer, Prayer during the Day, Night Prayer and the Book of Psalms. There are seasonal variations and provision for Saints and other 'Feast' days. Despite the helpful introduction, it is a bit complicated to use at first but an excellent and very full resource once you get used to it. Such 'Offices' are, of course, designed to be used with others, though many find them helpful to use on their own.

Time to Pray, also published by Church House. A beautifully produced, slim volume which includes Prayer during the Day (with seasonal variations) and Night Prayer. Some Psalms and some Bible readings are included. Ideal if you are travelling or if you prefer a simpler structure.

I struggled for years with books about prayer. However, I then discovered books of prayers, which, a bit like poetry, often expressed what I wanted to say but had no words for. I include a few I have found helpful. Some are out of print but are available second-hand from <www.amazon.co.uk> or <www.abebooks.co.uk>.

A Thousand Reasons for Living and other books of prayers and meditations by Helder Camara, DLT
An African Prayer Book, Desmond Tutu, Hodder and Stoughton, 1998
Approaches to Prayer, Henry Morgan, SPCK, 1991, reissued 2008
Bread for Tomorrow, Janet Morley, SPCK/Christian Aid, 2004
Common Prayer Collection, Michael Leunig, Collins Dove, 1993 (This looks like a children's book, but don't be fooled: it is profound)
God of Surprises, Gerard Hughes, DLT, 1985
Sadhana, A Way to God, Anthony de Mello, Doubleday, 1984
The Edge of Glory, Power Lines and other prayer collections by David Adam, SPCK
The Lion Prayer Collection, Mary Batchelor, Lion, 2001
The SPCK Book of Christian Prayer, SPCK, 2009

Websites

There are many websites offering daily prayer or meditation. Two excellent ones are:

www.rejesus.co.uk – daily prayer and other resources. An interdenominational organization supported by most major denominations with an evangelical leaning.

www.sacredspace.ie – daily meditations produced by Roman Catholic Jesuits in Ireland.

Sacred space

God is everywhere and we can speak and listen to God wherever we are. For many people, however, some places have become special, places where they find it particularly easy to be in touch with God. It may be a special room or chair in our homes. It may be a particular walk or a place by the sea or in the hills. It may also be a 'holy' place, a place where others have prayed for centuries. 'Holy', of course, does not mean 'having some special moral character'. It means 'set apart for a different use'. Some people call these 'thin places', places where earth and heaven seem to touch each other.

I travelled around Ireland a few years ago with a friend. It was a sort of pilgrimage healthily mixed with a spot of Guinness and some Irish whiskey tasting. We found ourselves, to our great surprise, standing in awe in ancient ruined chapels where the saints once prayed and touching holy stones. Perhaps in the West we have become too 'dualistic', separating off the physical from the spiritual, something quite alien to our Celtic forebears, and to the ancient Desert Fathers who influenced them. You see that interweaving of the spiritual and the physical in Celtic patterns carved on stone crosses and penned on ancient Gospel texts. Even today, in Eastern monasticism, there are regular accounts of two-way conversations and meetings with angels, saints and demons.[4] The monks talk about these encounters in such a matter-of-fact way that they seem interwoven into their daily lives. It is easy for us in the West to think this far-fetched. Yet perhaps is it we who have lost the immediacy and reality of the spiritual interwoven with the material world?

Having come to Ely from a church built in the 1960s, a multi-purpose square box with nothing aesthetically pleasing to commend it, I found Ely's magnificent cathedral speaking to me of God's presence. And it's not just me. Many of the tourists, coming to see the architecture, are suddenly transported to a place beyond themselves. The very scale of the building speaks of the majesty of God. Its majestic presence, towering over the Fens for almost a thousand years, puts into perspective our own brief lives. Like Jacob, we find ourselves saying: 'How awesome is this place. This is none other than the house of God. This is the gateway of heaven.'[5]

Furthermore, we may find ourselves encouraged, spurred on, by the saints of old who knelt and worshipped in this very place, whom we see portrayed in paint, stone, wood and glass. Reciting the creed every week and saying 'I believe in the Communion of Saints' meant little to me for years. But here, sitting under the Octagon, thinking of the great heroes of the faith who also prayed here in Ely, it becomes much more real: Etheldreda and her sisters, Dunstan, Athelwold, Simeon, Alan de Walsingham, Lancelot Andrewes, and many others whose names we do not know. 'Since we are surrounded by so great a cloud of witnesses,' says the writer of the letter to the Hebrews, 'let us lay aside every weight, and the sin which clings to us so closely, and run with perseverance the race that is set before us, looking to Jesus, the pioneer and perfecter of our faith.'[6] I can imagine them, spurring us on, encouraging us, supporting us with their prayers. After all, why should they cease to be concerned for us, just because they are dead?

My brother, an avowed atheist, came to visit us shortly after we moved to Ely. He popped over to look at the building and came back a couple of hours later looking stunned. 'Well,' he said, 'all I can say is, that was a spiritual experience.'

Finding a spiritual place, a place in which we can be still, a place, perhaps, where others have prayed down the centuries, a place that quietens our minds and draws us God-ward, can often be a great help as we seek to listen to God. For me, for example, sitting still, on my own, can be torture. Yet doing something physical, even if it's only doodling, allows me to focus more clearly. And when I am sitting by a river or the sea or in front of a blazing fire, somehow the movement of the water and the flames allows me to be still.

What we find helpful will depend on the sort of people we are. It may be more than one place. It may be a corner of a room, made special by putting a cross or a picture on the wall or by lighting a candle. There may be a special place to which we go every week and perhaps somewhere we travel to occasionally on retreat. It may be the local park or the treadmill at the gym, or even, as it is for some people, the loo! Wherever and whatever it is, it is worth seeking a place which, for us, is holy, a sacred space, regularly accessible to us, set apart for the special purpose of listening to God.

Exercise

1 What are the places which help you to be still, to pray, to feel close to God?

2 Do you find the place where you normally pray helpful? If not, is it possible for you to change the place where you pray? What can you do to create a 'sacred space' somewhere in your own home?

3 What particular 'holy' places might you explore?

Listening to God through the Bible

I am leading a Bible-study group in La Paz, Bolivia. We are working our way through the book of Exodus. I explain how, after Joseph died, the Hebrews have multiplied and become a threat to the Egyptians. So, one of the Pharaohs, centuries later, begins to treat them like slaves. Finally, God calls Moses to set them free. Wanting to focus on God's faithfulness, I ask the question: 'What do we learn about God from the fact that, after so many years, he called Moses to set his people free?' There is a pause, then Alfonso chips in: 'Well,' he says, 'it shows God didn't really care about them at all, since he forgot them for hundreds of years.'

It is easy, for those of us who have studied theology, to forget how very difficult much of the Bible is. Easy, too, for us to avoid the clear implication of what some of the Bible says, as we try to mould the meaning into our preconceived ideas of what God *ought* to be like. It is not surprising that, in Britain, even among worshipping Christians, the practice of Bible reading has gradually diminished. Parts of the Old Testament offer a picture of God which is ill at ease with our modern mindset. Indeed, it sometimes paints him as a despotic tyrant.

Yet it is astonishing how much of our Western literature and art takes for granted a knowledge of the Bible. A few years ago I was in a poetry-reading group, run by our local university. I was surprised to find that I was the only one to pick up the clear, biblical allusions, not just in seventeenth-century poetry, but in the modern poets as well. Just look at the poems of Wilfred Owen or the paintings of Francis Bacon or the novels of Jeanette Winterson. Getting to grips with the Bible, apart from its potential spiritual value, has the added benefit of helping us understand our own culture and history better. So, how can we begin to get to grips with it?

Keith Ward, in a recent book, offers a helpful way of thinking about how we can understand the Bible:

> The Bible is a collection of human responses to what were felt to be encounters with God in the history of Israel and in the dreams, visions, and oracles of the prophets. Its various documents are mixtures of insight and prejudice, moving poetic evocations of transcendence and ugly expressions of human vindictiveness and petty-mindedness. Overall, however, the Bible shows a series of developing insights into the nature of God as the one creator of beauty and perfection, who has a moral goal for the human world, and who relates to human lives with a mixture of categorical moral demand, forgiving compassion and the promise of ultimate hope for human fulfilment. It is one of the fullest and most complete accounts of the development of a human religious tradition, over many centuries. It shows how contemporary religious believers have come to be where they are.'[7]

The Bible is God's gradual revelation of himself to us in history, interpreted and written down by human beings. Some of it is hard to understand. Some of the Old Testament, in particular, attributes actions to God, such as ethnic cleansing, that today we would consider utterly abhorrent. For example, according to 1 Samuel 15, God is angry with Saul and rejects him as king, because he has not done a thorough enough job of slaughtering all the Amalekites, including the women, children and animals. Such action is completely out of keeping with the God we see revealed in Christ.

On the other hand, much of the Bible is utterly inspiring. It is therefore important that we read the difficult passages in the light of those more easily understood and, in particular, read everything in the light of the Gospels, which speak of God's ultimate and definitive revelation of himself in Jesus Christ. It is no wonder that, in so much of our Christian heritage, the reading of the Gospel assumes the very highest importance in the liturgy. With this in mind, if we are just starting to read the Bible, it is clearly best to start with the Gospels, rather than getting bogged down in Numbers and Leviticus.

It may also be helpful to use a Bible-reading scheme, so that we receive some help in understanding and avoid simply looking at our favourite passages, which brings the danger of losing a sense of balance and breadth in our approach.

But the purpose of Bible reading is not simply gaining knowledge: it is about allowing God to speak to us and to lead us increasingly into the likeness of Christ; it is about the formation of our lives.

The psalmist asks:

> How can the young person keep their way pure?
> By living according to your word.

I have stored up your word in my heart, that I might not
  sin against you.

Ps. 119.9–11

The psalmist is *not* saying: 'I've memorized the Bible so that, when faced with a tricky issue, I can remember what to do.' Rather, he is saying: 'As I read and digest God's word, it becomes so much part of my being that loving and serving God and neighbour become the natural flow of my life.'

However, let us not underrate memorization, which seems to be much less important to us in these days of portable technology, at least in the West. (Note the contrast, for example, with the importance of memorization of the Qur'an in Islam.) Memorizing Scripture, liturgy and, indeed, poetry, allows us to access the text without the need for books.

It is often in times of crisis that such words – words that are somehow deep within us, yet also beyond us – come to the surface. Fergal Keane speaks of walking towards a church after the Rwanda genocide of 1994. As he approaches there is the terrible stench of death, severed limbs, heads, hacked body-parts of children, lying in the grass. 'I begin to pray myself,' he says, '"Our Father, who art in heaven . . ." These are words I have not said since my childhood, but I need them now.'[8]

I have been with people suffering severe dementia, unable to recognize others but loudly singing well-known hymns. Or sitting with a dying person who can still recite Psalm 23 or join in the Lord's Prayer. These are not superficial things. They are about what remains of us when everything else is stripped away. To 'hear, read, mark, learn and inwardly digest',[9] particularly Scripture, but also liturgy and holy text, is about the formation of our lives.

There are a number of ways we might do this. We have already thought about the 'Daily Office', including the reciting of Psalms and liturgy (much of which is based on Scripture anyway), which, over the years, sticks in our memory. Ignatian spirituality, for example, invites us to use our imagination to identify ourselves with the different characters in biblical stories. Evangelical spirituality asks us not just to understand the meaning but it also challenges us to apply the lessons in our daily lives. The Benedictine tradition offers us 'Lectio Divina', a slow, reflective, imaginative reading of Scripture, dwelling on a word or phrase that strikes us, allowing it to roll around in our mouth and heart and to enter deeply into us. It is less concerned about understanding the whole passage than about allowing some part of the text to speak to us. Classically 'Lectio' has five movements:

1 *Silencio.* Quiet stilling of the heart and mind.
2 *Lectio.* Reading the passage slowly, aloud, lingering over a word or phrase that catches our attention.
3 *Meditatio.* A second reading of the passage, this time listening for what God might be saying to us.
4 *Oratio.* A third reading, responding to the passage in prayer.
5 *Contemplatio.* Resting, waiting, contemplating in the presence of God, allowing time for the Word to sink deep into our soul.

This approach can be applied to other devotional books as well as the Bible.[10]

Other traditions use daily Bible-reading schemes, often with notes on the passage set for the day. Whatever method we choose (and we may find it refreshing to change what we do from time to time), the Bible is the fundamental document of our faith, and we neglect it to our own great loss.

Resources

Daily Bible-reading notes. A number of organizations publish these. Many are now free online. They offer a systematic approach to Bible reading and include helpful explanations as well as comments and questions that help us apply what we read to our own lives. Two well worth exploring are:

Bible Reading Fellowship – www.biblereadingnotes.org.uk

Scripture Union – www.scriptureunion.org.uk or directly to www. wordlive.org

BRF and Scripture Union both offer a number of different resources for different ages, stages and in different styles, online and in hard copy format. See also the online daily worship resources (above).

Introduction to the Bible. Recommended reading:

The Lion Handbook to the Bible, Lion, 2004. A great resource for beginners including sections on history, culture, language, geography, and lots of illustrations.

The Word of God? The Bible after Modern Scholarship, Keith Ward, SPCK, 2010.

Bible versions. There are a great many different 'translations' (from the original Hebrew and Greek texts) available. It is often helpful to refer to more than one version in order to try and capture the meaning of a passage or see it in a new way.

Good News Bible. A translation that tries to capture the overall meaning using everyday modern language.

New Revised Standard Version. A fairly literal, word-for-word, modern translation.

The 100 Minute Bible, Michael Hinton, Chronicle, 2007. A very brief summary of some of the main stories, psalms, parables, events of the Bible. A great place to start.

The Book of God, Walter Wangarin Jnr, Lion Hudson, 1998. The Bible retold as a novel from start to finish.

The Message Bible, Eugene Peterson. A paraphrase version that majors on accessible language rather literal translation.

Praying the Psalms

As already mentioned, praying the Psalms is at the heart of the Benedictine daily pattern of worship. The Psalms are the Bible's hymn book and prayer book. They often strike us as beautiful poetry. Many of them are very familiar to us, such as Psalm 23.

> The LORD is my shepherd; I shall not want.
> He maketh me to lie down in green pastures: he leadeth me beside the still waters.
> He restoreth my soul: he leadeth me in the paths of righteousness for his name's sake.
> Yea, though I walk through the valley of the shadow of death, I will fear no evil: for thou art with me; thy rod and thy staff they comfort me.
> Thou preparest a table before me in the presence of mine enemies: thou anointest my head with oil; my cup runneth over.
> Surely goodness and mercy shall follow me all the days of my life: and I will dwell in the house of the LORD for ever.[11]

Like the old advert for the *News of the World*: 'All human life is there', the Psalms display every kind of emotion. There is joy, contentment, love, passion, hope, faithfulness, longing, gratitude, celebration, devotion, praise. And there is also anger, bitterness, guilt, blame, despair, abandonment, betrayal, fear, envy, thirst for revenge. They assure us, should we be in any doubt, that whatever we feel, no matter how shocking, we can express it to God – even our bitterness, frustration and anger at God himself. (See, for example, Psalms 88 and 137.)

Walter Brueggemann[12] offers us a structure which can help us pray the Psalms. He says there are essentially three types of psalms.

1 Psalms of Orientation. These form the bedrock of our belief. They speak of the things which hold us firm, the solid ground on which we stand. For example, Psalm 1.1–3: 'Happy are those . . . whose delight is in the LORD. They are like trees planted by streams of water . . . in all that they do they prosper.' Or Psalm 91.1–2: 'You who live in the shelter of the Most High, who abide in the shadow of the Almighty, will say to the LORD: 'My refuge and my fortress; my God in whom I trust.'

2 Psalms of Dis-orientation. Typically these follow an experience of trouble, disappointment or tragedy, when all our certainty is swept away and we are left wounded, hurt, bereft. Suddenly, what we thought we believed is completely at odds with our experience, and we are left floundering. For example, Psalm 44.17–23: 'All this has come upon us though we have not forgotten you or been false to your covenant . . . Rouse yourself! Why are you asleep O Lord? Awake! Do not cast us off for ever.' Or Psalm 22.1–2: 'My God, my God, why have you forsaken me?' – words recited by Jesus on the cross. Indeed, says Brueggemann, in New Testament terms these are 'Psalms of the cross'. They mark that place of despair and defeat where we cry out to God but receive no reply. They also speak of the plight of those who suffer 'the daily distress of being alive'.[13]

3 Psalms of New Orientation. But then, says Brueggemann, something happens. It is as though the sun suddenly breaks through the clouds on a dreary day. God's grace touches us. The circumstances may not have changed, but we are changed. We are able to see things in a new light, from a 'new orientation'. Psalm 96.1–2 says: 'O sing to the LORD a new song, sing to the LORD all the earth. Sing to the LORD, bless his name, tell of his salvation from day to day.' Such psalms, in New Testament terms, are psalms of resurrection.

This is an ongoing cycle, reflecting our different moods and experiences – and God's grace in our lives. At different times, different psalms will speak to us in these different ways. We can use them not just to reflect our own situation but to identify with others as well. So, for example, a psalm of betrayal might become our prayer for someone who has been betrayed by a partner; a psalm that cries out for revenge, our identification with the woman raped or the people driven from their homes in Sudan; a psalm that is a song of thanks – for the couple who've just had a baby. Hence the Bible's prayer book can become ours, too.

Exercise

1 Write your own Psalm of *Orientation*, using the refrain from Psalm 136.

> ¹ O give thanks to the LORD for he is good,
> His steadfast love endures for ever.
> ² O give thanks to the God of gods,
> His steadfast love endures for ever.
> ³ O give thanks to the Lord of lords,
> His steadfast love endures for ever.

O give thanks to the Lord for . . . .
His steadfast love endures for ever.

O give thanks to the Lord for . . . .
His steadfast love endures for ever.

O give thanks to the Lord for . . . .
His steadfast love endures for ever. (*etc.*)

2 Write your own psalm of *disorientation*, of complaint, of lament, of anger, based on Psalm 22.

> ¹ My God, my God, why have you forsaken me?
> Why are you so far from helping me, from the words of
>   my groaning?

² O my God, I cry by day, but you do not answer;
and by night, but find no rest.

. . . .

My God, my God, why have you forsaken me?

. . . .

My God, my God, why have you forsaken me? (*etc.*)

3 Write your own psalm of *new orientation*, of resurrection, of
being touched by God's grace once more, based on Psalm 96.

¹ O sing to the LORD a new song; sing to the Lord, all the
  earth.
² Sing to the Lord, bless his name; tell of his salvation
  from day to day.
³ Declare his glory among the nations, his marvellous
  works among all the peoples.

. . . . O sing to the Lord a new song, sing to the Lord,
all the earth.

. . . . O sing to the Lord a new song, sing to the Lord,
all the earth. (*etc.*)

Listening to others

Primo Levi, a Jewish Holocaust survivor, wrote, after the war,
a first-hand account of life in a concentration camp. He speaks,
at one point, about the regular, arbitrary selection: some for
the gas chamber and some to survive. As they cram back into
the hut, knowing their fate, waiting for the death-call in the
morning, Kuhn, an elderly man, rocks back and forth as he
thanks God aloud for sparing his life. He is quite oblivious to
the grief of the younger men around him, men with families
and children, who are destined, tomorrow, for the gas chamber.
Levi is incensed by Kuhn's inability to hear the anguish of his

own, younger, cellmates. 'If I were God,' he says, 'I would spit on Kuhn's prayer.'[14] Prayer that is only about my own needs and concerns is a long way from engaging with the heart of God and responding to the world's cry.

David, a good friend of ours, was born and brought up in northern Argentina, where his parents were missionaries and where he himself returned to work as a missionary. One morning he was packing the truck to leave for a visit to some isolated villages when Ernesto, one of the Toba people, someone David had grown up with in the village – a friend since childhood – came to visit. They exchanged greetings and asked about each other's families. David then asked Ernesto if there was anything he needed, anything he could do for him. 'No,' replied Ernesto. 'I just popped over to say hello.' 'Are you sure,' responded David, 'because I can easily do this trip another day if it's something important.' But Ernesto insisted he was OK. So, after another few minutes of conversation, David drove off in the truck.

When he returned that evening he discovered, to his horror, that Ernesto's daughter had died the previous evening and they had buried her that day. Ernesto had come to ask David to do the funeral. Why hadn't he told David? Because Ernesto could see that David was in a rush. That he didn't really have time. And this was something far too important to speak of, unless you were absolutely sure you had full attention.

Initially I thought that story demonstrated the huge cultural gulf between us and the indigenous people of northern Argentina, despite David's own intimate knowledge of them. Yet, as I have thought about it over the years, it seems to me that this sort of thing happens all the time in our Western world, too. I think of the woman who mentioned to me, in passing, that her neighbour was not too well and, if I had time, could I pop in and see him? The way she mentioned it, in passing, didn't seem urgent, so I didn't give it a big priority. But it turned out he was on the brink of death, and I arrived too late. Or the many occasions when, at the end of a pastoral visit, I say a prayer and stand up to leave. But as I am half-way out of the door they meekly say: 'Oh by the way . . .' And then, if I turn and give them my full attention, the real business comes out. I wonder how many times I have left without it ever crossing their lips?

Some years ago I was driving, in the early summer after the first rains, from the Argentine Chaco to the provincial capital, Salta. Cattle crossed the road, leaving their cow-pats on the tarmac. On these cow-pats settled not one or two but thousands upon thousands of butterflies. As the truck sped over them they flew up and were instantly welded on to the radiator. Every few miles the engine would overheat as the radiator ceased to function, so I had to keep on getting out to scrape the radiator clean. It was a messy job. So, I carefully removed my Omega watch, a twenty-first-birthday present from my long-dead grandma, and laid it at the side of the road, putting it on again when the task was finished. On one such occasion I must have forgotten to pick it up again. I only realized 200 miles later when I arrived in Salta and looked at my wrist to find out the time. It was, of course, not there. I travelled back on the same road the following day, but it had gone.

However, over the following weeks I noticed something remarkable. People were speaking to me more freely, sharing more deeply. I realized that, when I had the watch, I would look at it, involuntarily, every few minutes. My glances at the watch seemed to send out the message: 'I really haven't got time for you. I have more important things to be doing.' I have never worn a wrist-watch from that day.

Our inability or unwillingness to listen is betrayed in many subtle ways. People need to know that we have their full attention – like Job's friends in the Bible. The best thing they did for Job was to sit with him in silence.

> They sat with him on the ground for seven days and seven nights and no one spoke a word to him, for they saw that his suffering was very great.

Once they started talking to him, however, they began to make his troubles even more unbearable.[15]

People often say, after a death, 'I'd like to go and visit but I don't know what to say.' The truth is, what we say, unless we say something really crass, is of far less importance than the fact that we went – or didn't go. And simply to be present with another person in grief or pain, without saying anything, can be a huge help in itself.

Part of our difficulty is that we live in a 'can do' society. We expect that, if we make the right choices, get the right advice, do the right thing, all will be well. Unfortunately that is far from true. Even in places like the UK people suffer serious accidents, untimely death, their marriage breaks down, their son develops cancer or becomes mentally ill, they lose their job and can't pay the mortgage. These things are not anomalies. They represent normal life, alongside all the good things life holds for us. Often we can do very little to help practically. Yet we can listen, be fully present, attentive, alert not just to words but to hands and eyes as well. 'Often secrets are not revealed in words. They lie concealed in the silence between the words or in the depth of what is unsayable between two people.'[16] Helder Camara, former Archbishop of Recife in Brazil, puts it this way: 'Between being shade, giving shade and casting shade, lie gulfs over which God alone can guide us.'[17]

To listen is to feel some of what the other person is feeling; to share the pain with them, which means carrying some of the burden for them ourselves. It is not about telling them our

'Anam Cara' Soulfriend

own story, how we had an experience just like theirs. It is about paying close attention to *their* story. This is true listening. Which is why, when we have really 'been there' for someone, we often feel so drained, as if, like Jesus, the 'power has gone out' of us.[18] Whereas they may well feel relieved, as if their burden has lightened. This is a great gift to be able to offer, something well worth nurturing. It is a meaningful engagement which has a healing character. It is quite different from offering advice. And you do not have to be a professional therapist to do it.

My fifth-form school report from my chemistry teacher, Mr Gittings, says: 'Able but idle.' I think that applies to my listening as well. I know I *can* do it, but so often the need to listen occurs not in a pre-planned pastoral visit but as an aside to an apparently ordinary encounter. So I find myself in a different frame of mind. I am too full of myself. Too much into the banter. Too eager to butt in with: '. . . and let me tell you about when that happened to me', thus taking the attention away from the one needing to be listened to. Or else I am keen to be somewhere else, eager to get away, which is obvious from my demeanour. So I fail to pick up what is important or offer any real support.

On the other hand, the times when I know I've *really* listened, people often say: 'Thank you so much. You've been such a help. Thank you.' This most often occurs when I've said almost nothing, when I haven't given any advice at all. In fact, listening has very little to do with offering advice. It is no wonder that counselling and other similar therapies are flourishing in the West. We are so busy, our minds so full of competing stuff that, in the normal course of life, we do not have the space for someone else's stuff as well. Yet to feel that you have really been listened to, fully heard, to have someone pick up the hint you drop and find out what is really troubling you, that is a most affirming and empowering experience.

Listen

One day Di, a retired cleaner, informed me that she couldn't come to the Bible-study group any more. Di didn't say much in the group, which was unfortunately dominated by someone with a classics degree, who kept wanting to know what the original Greek said. But when Di did speak it was pithy and down to earth, rooted in daily experience. I was about to reply, 'That's OK, Di, don't worry.' Yet something inside me made me pause, and say instead, 'Well, that's fine if you really can't make it, Di, but actually I'd be really sorry if you couldn't come, because what you say makes us face the real issues, rather than just having a theoretical discussion.' Her face lit up. 'Oh,' she said, 'do you really think so? The thing is, I *love* coming, but I thought you didn't really want me because I'm not very clever.'

Listening to others goes well beyond 'pastoral encounters'. It is about our relationships with family, friends and work colleagues. It is about how we make decisions in business, in community groups or in church. Our ability to be attentive to others, particularly if we are in positions of authority, is vital to the success of our enterprise, whatever that may be.

Our listening is not just in order that we may understand what the other is saying or feeling. It is also about giving a voice to those who find it hard to articulate what they are thinking or feeling, people like Ernesto and Di, who need time, space, encouragement and our undivided attention to be able to share what's on their hearts.

Regarding the meeting of the Taizé Community Council, the Rule says: 'The first step is to establish silence in oneself so as to prepare to listen to one's Lord.'[19] Listening to God is not unrelated to how we listen to others, since it is often through others that God speaks to us. And the reasons we find it hard to listen to others are often the same reasons we find it hard to listen to God as well. We are too restless, too keen to be getting on with our busy schedule, too keen to get our point across, too full of our own agenda to have space for anything else. And the danger is that 'without deep experience of God . . . we will end up speaking only about ourselves'.[20]

Which is why we need silence.

Exercise

When you are sitting talking with someone make a mental note of the following:

1 What percentage of the time were *they* talking and what percentage were *you* talking?

2 When they were talking, what were you thinking about? Were you concentrating on what they were saying and trying to identify with it or did it just trigger off a similar experience in you that you couldn't wait to talk about?

3 Did you give this person your full attention or were you distracted by other things going on in your mind?

4 How many times did you look at your watch? Never? Once? Often? Did it have any noticeable effect on the communication?

5 Were you able to clear your mind to listen but at the same time retain a balanced outlook? You may have had a train to catch or a child to pick up from school, which you clearly needed to attend to?

6 How did you end the conversation? Were you able to end it in such a way as to keep the possibility of dialogue open?

Silence

Theophilus of holy memory, Bishop of Alexandria, journeyed to Skete, and the brethren coming together said to Abba Pambo:

'Say a word or two to the Bishop that his soul may be edified in this place.' The Elder replied: 'If he is not edified by my silence there is no hope he will be edified by my words.'[21]

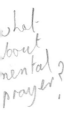

How difficult it is for most of us to be silent. As I start each day, sitting in the chapel, waiting for Morning Prayer to begin, my mind is already racing forward into the day ahead. I am too distracted, too geared up for the day's work, to enter deeply into prayer or concentrate on a reading or, more importantly, simply be still. I need other opportunities during the year when I can give myself the time to become quiet inside.

Although they are important, I find I cannot develop a balanced life simply on a diet of *daily* prayer and worship. So each year I try and do a couple of things. First, I try and go somewhere I can receive stimulating input from others, outside my own work context. For me it is probably Greenbelt, a Christian Arts Festival held over the August Bank Holiday weekend in Cheltenham. But it could be Spring Harvest, New Wine, Taizé, Iona, Walsingham or whatever you personally find most helpful.[22] There is a balance to be struck here between settling into a regular and familiar rhythm and simply finding PLUs – 'people like us' – who just reinforce our own viewpoint and offer us no challenge or new perspective.

However, I need something else as well. I need silence. And silence, for me at least, is not something I can enter into quickly. It takes me a few days. So I try and take at least three or four days each year in silent retreat. There are lots of retreat places to choose from, many of them associated with religious communities. *Retreats*, a journal published annually in December, not only lists the ones in the UK but has a short introduction that gives you a feel for each place. In such places there often seems to exist a prayerfulness and stillness which is not of my own creation but into which I am invited.

43

When I arrive it is always the same pattern. The first couple of days I spend fretting about all the urgent things I am not doing, the issues that worry me, the decisions that have to be made, the difficult conversation that awaits my return, the emails I haven't replied to (and which are piling up by the minute as I sit there). If necessary, I make a note of these issues, so I know I won't forget them when I get back. I can then put them to one side for the time being. I am also generally exhausted, so I sleep a lot. And then, after a couple of days, to use a helpful phrase of my wife, I 'come to the end of my thoughts'. When this happens I begin to be still. I cease to be so preoccupied with the busy-ness of my daily life at home and at work. I become more open to God and I begin to get in touch with the really important stuff that is buried deep inside me, but which rarely has a chance to surface.

A few years ago I went on retreat and, as usual, found on the first couple of days my mind buzzing. But then, on day three, as I began to enter into the silence, I found myself in touch with what was deep within me, which turned out to be the very raw feelings of grief over the death of my dad, eight months earlier. The trouble was that after my dad died my mum was so needy I spent all my spare energy looking out for her. So it was only in the silence of the retreat that I became aware of just how much I missed him. And I was able, in the silence, to think of him, and weep.

Often, what we discover within ourselves when we finally become silent is painful or uncomfortable. The great writers also tell us that silence is the place where nothing happens, where there is no answer to our prayer, where God himself is silent. It is not surprising that many of us try and block it out with the noise of the iPod, computer screen, games console or TV. 'Who does not fear silence and prefer diversion?'[23] Yet it is in those recesses of our inner self that our real work with God

Rule of Taize

So you think we should look at "Rule of Taizé

and with our own souls takes place. That is why all the great spiritual writers insist upon it as a major discipline. As Christopher Jamison, Abbot of Worth Abbey, says, it is the place where we must confront our inner demons. Rowan Williams, speaking of the Desert Fathers, says: 'If there is one virtue pretty universally recommended in the desert, it is this: Silence.'[24] He goes on: 'without silence we shall not get any closer to knowing who we are before God.' The Rule of Taizé tells us: 'In the solitude of a retreat we are renewed by intimate meeting with Christ.'[25]

Taizé

For many of us the idea of spending time in silence is a difficult prospect – frightening even. If you are just starting, it is worth looking out for organized 'quiet days' or short, guided retreats where you can find help to discover how to cope with silence and gradually grow into it.

Far from removing us from the real world, silence often enables people to be more acutely aware of the world and its troubles and to be better at listening than those of us who are full of 'background noise'. Silence is for a purpose, as the Taizé Rule reminds us: 'Let there be no useless asceticism. Gaining mastery of yourself has no aim other than to render you more available.'[26]

Silence can also be a place of healing and reconciliation. Brother Roger of Taizé says: 'If you can't agree, pray together. If you can't agree about the words, pray in silence.'

stress to each other

It was in the silence where the Desert Fathers found themselves battling their demons. It is in the silence where we will find ourselves battling ours.

Exercise *Being alone — at home —*

1 What is your experience of silence? Is it something you find difficult? If so, why?   *No*

2 Talk about your experience of silence with friends/cell group/ soul friend. What have others found helpful? What can you

Like a painter — a dancers life is silent — practice + practice.

learn from them? What might you do with others to explore silence together? *B. Study*

3 If you have not had much experience of being in silence before, why not book a quiet day at a local retreat centre?

4 If you have already spent a day or so in silence, why not contemplate a longer period, several days perhaps, of silent retreat?

Speaking

If Benedict is very strict on the subject of speaking, he is even more damning when it comes to laughter. 'But as for loose talk, idle words and talk that stimulates laughter, we condemn this with a permanent ban in all places.'[27] This is very bad news for me as I am a born talker and a great joker! Luckily, I can remind myself that I am not called to the religious life. Yet I do well to think seriously about what this means. Anyone who has spent more than a couple of days in complete silence will know the experience of coming out of silence. One of the things that always strikes me is how superficial most of our conversation is. Much of what I say when engaging socially is, if I am honest, banal.

And humour? I do wonder if Benedict didn't miss something important about the great value of humour and the healing power of laughter? However, it is also true that a great deal of humour is at the expense of others. Benedict is not alone in condemning this. 'Buffoonery has never renewed joy,' says Brother Roger.[28] It can be insensitive, cruel even, as all those who have been on the wrong end of it will know. Re-reading the letter of James provides a timely reminder of the potential destructiveness of speech. 'Let everyone be quick to listen and slow to speak.'[29]

The issue of what we might call 'right speaking' is a major one in the Bible, as well as for Benedict. Perhaps his strongest and most frequent condemnation is of 'murmuring', 'grumbling' or 'complaining'.[30] Sadly, such speech is endemic in our society, including the Church. Paradoxically, the more we have the more demanding and dissatisfied we seem to become. We feel unfairly treated, cheated, unhappy about a decision that didn't go our way, demanding a refund because the product didn't quite meet our expectations, needing to defend or justify ourselves, envious of another's position, keen to repay a perceived wrong, wanting to get others on our side, eager to cut someone down to size.

We see this not just in our own context but also in the Bible. The disciples grumble about James and John's desire for promotion[31] and about the money wasted on the ointment used to anoint Jesus.[32] The monks grumble about perceived unfair treatment or impossible demands.

Interestingly, Benedict is quite clear that people are *not* all to be treated equally. They are to be treated according to ability, according to holiness of life and especially according to need. Hence weaker brethren will be assigned lighter work. The sick may receive extra food. The person who is most trustworthy rather than the one who is most able or senior may be made responsible for the monastery's goods. The one noted for holy living rather than the person from a wealthy family may become the Prior. Benedict does allow monks to speak with their superiors if they feel the demands upon them are too great.[33] But what he doesn't allow under any circumstances is background grumbling or gossip. St James exhorts us:

> The tongue is a restless evil, full of deadly poison. With it we bless our Lord and Father and with it we curse those who are made in the likeness of God. Brothers and sisters, this ought not to be so.[34]

To give an example of just how serious this is, the Greek word used for 'malicious gossip' in 1 Timothy 3.11 is *'diabolos'*, the same word that is used for the devil himself!

How can we escape from this danger? Here are four 'rules of thumb' you may find helpful.

First, as we have already seen, *restraint*. St Paul tells us: 'All things are lawful, but not all things are beneficial.'[35] Do I really need to say it? Will it help? Is it more likely to build up or break down; do good or do harm? Would it be better for me just to keep my trap shut – at least until I've thought about it a bit more?

Second, if it really needs saying, *speak openly*. We need to learn to speak straightforwardly, face to face, to the person concerned, rather than behind their back. Inability to speak plainly to one another seems to be a peculiarly British disease. I once attended, as an observer, the Synod of the Episcopal Church of Spain. I was shocked to see people standing up and shouting at each other across the room. It seemed to me quite un-Christian. However, by the evening they had all got it off their chests and were able to sit down and relax with each other, chatting, enjoying paella and drinking wine together.

A former colleague told me of an ecumenical meeting between German Lutherans and English Anglicans. At one point the discussions started to become rather heated. The Anglican Bishop who was chairing the session suggested this might be a good moment to break for a cup of tea. One of the Germans stood up, banged his fist on the table and shouted: 'That's the trouble with you English. You can't bear to face conflict. Let's stay until we've thrashed it out!' I can think of many church meetings I've attended where a cross word was never spoken in public, but where people left fuming, grumbling to each other in private. If it is not dealt with openly it may rumble on indefinitely. 'Speak the truth in love,' says St Paul. 'Putting away all falsehood let us all speak the truth to our neighbours. Be angry but do not fall into sin. Do not let the sun go down on your anger and do not make room for the devil.'[36] *Ephesians*

Rowan Williams talks about finding 'a way to speak that resonates with the creative word working in their depths', resonating perhaps with the 'harmonics hidden in that primal sound . . . of the first eternal word'.[37] Lest we think this is fanciful religious language, mathematicians are using similar language about the 'harmonics' or 'drumbeat' of the universe, which, astonishingly, seems to link the sequence of prime numbers to quantum mechanics, chaos theory, DNA sequencing, and even the properties of glass – what Marcus de Sautoy calls 'the Music of the Primes'.[38] We often talk about being 'on a wavelength' with someone, that something someone has said 'resonates' with us or that there is 'chemistry' between us. We may call it intuition, or the discernment of the Holy Spirit. Whatever it is, it is worth seeking, so that we may find a way to resonate with people, instead of clashing in awkward disharmony, as we seek to speak the truth in love.

Third, *speak kindly*. St Benedict speaks of the role of the Cellarer, the monk called to look after the goods of the monastery. If he is met with unreasonable demands or is unable to provide someone with what he seeks, 'he should not upset him by showing contempt . . . he should at least offer a kind word.'[39] In this context it is worth thinking of what people are able to bear. I think of my elderly mum, suffering from dementia. I would ask her how she was and she would tell me her sister Lily had just been to see her. At first I would remind her that Aunty Lily had died three years previously. 'Oh no,' she would cry, 'not Lily!' And she would burst into tears as she began to relive the grief again, as if for the first time. I soon discovered that it was kinder just to nod. This is, however, an extreme case. We need to beware of using 'speaking kindly' as an excuse for not speaking honestly and openly.

Finally, and most importantly, we need to *be aware of our own faults and failings* before we rush off to sort other people out. This is not the same as being consumed by guilt: it is about viewing ourselves with humility and not setting ourselves up in judgement over others. 'Why do you see the speck in your neighbour's eye but fail to notice the log in your own eye?' asks Jesus.[40] 'Do not judge and you will not be judged. Do not condemn and you will not be condemned. Forgive and you will be forgiven. Give, and it will be given to you, full measure, pressed down, shaken together and running over . . . for the measure you give will be the measure you get back.'[41]

The *Wisdom of the Desert*[42] tells us of a monk who came to Abbot Sisois, livid after being insulted by another monk and determined to get revenge. After failing to persuade him to forgive, the Abbot prayed thus: 'O God, you are no longer necessary to us and we no longer need you . . . since, as our brother says, we can and will avenge ourselves.' The monk, hearing the prayer, at last began to realize the implication of what he was saying and gave up his quest for revenge.

To judge others, to fail to forgive, is to put ourselves in the place of God. And forgiveness is not just about telling someone we forgive them, which can be a great arrogance, since it assumes they, and not we, are in the wrong. It is about an attitude that offers forgiveness and acceptance before it is asked for, that takes the initiative in going to meet the other rather than waiting with arms crossed, saying to ourselves: 'Well, it's up to her. It's her problem. If she wants to come here and say sorry, then I'll forgive her.' The parable of the prodigal son, with the father rushing out to meet the son before he has even arrived, offers us a very different picture. At that stage, for all the father knows, the son might be coming back just to cadge more money. Yet his father does not wait to find out. Instead he runs to meet his son and embraces him before he even has a chance to speak.[43]

The offer of God's love, acceptance and forgiveness always precedes our response to it, and it provides us with a model of how we can live – and speak.

I write this for my own instruction. When it comes to 'right speaking' I have a very long way to go indeed.

yes, agree, extremely difficult

Resources

Holy Listening, Margaret Guenther, DLT, 1992.
Listening, Anne Long, DLT, 1990.
Listening to God, Joyce Huggett, Hodder and Stoughton, 1986.

Obedience

Most people called to the religious life, including the Benedictines, take vows of obedience. Obedience, like discipline, is not a popular concept these days. We like to think of ourselves as liberated from subservience. And indeed for many, such as women in the Western world, freedom from 'obedience' has been truly liberating. Yet it is easy to misunderstand the nature of obedience. Esther de Waal tells us that: 'obedience is derived from *oboedire*, which shares its roots with *audire*, to hear.'[44] Hence the word means 'to hear and then act upon what we have heard' or 'to listen deeply'. In Benedict's words it means to listen with 'the ear of your heart'.[45] Obedience is a natural consequence of deep and serious listening. We see the opposite of this with exasperated parents saying to their teenage kids: 'Have you listened to a word I've said?' The answer, presumably, is 'no', which means there is little chance of the parents' desired outcome. Though you do sometimes wonder if the parents have ever listened to the teenagers, either.

Obedience is, ultimately, to God. But it is also to those who have authority over us. However, obedience is not perceived as simply obeying the abbot or the person in authority. It is much more radical than that. It is about mutual submission, about considering the other person before ourselves. On the night before he dies, Jesus finds his disciples arguing over who is the greatest. 'The kings of the nations lord it over them,' Jesus tells them, 'but not so with you. Rather the greatest among you must become like the least and the leader the one who serves.'[46] And he gives them an example to follow by taking a bowl of water and a towel and washing their feet, the job for the lowliest servant.[47]

This brings us face to face with the great question: Who am I living for? What is the purpose of my life? Increasingly, it seems, *we* are our own centre of our lives. My decisions are all about what feels right to *me*, what *my* goals and plans are, how *I* see my future panning out, what *I* want to get out of life. Doing your own thing 'because you're worth it.'[48] I remember speaking to a man by the river in Cambridge. He had just retired and was planning to spend the next few years cruising the English canal system on his narrowboat. He spoke with pride of how he had had the boat built to his exact specifications; how he had carefully planned their routes for the next three years; how his well-planned retirement investments were making this possible; how he was not worried about anyone else because he and his wife were determined to enjoy themselves. As I heard him speak it reminded me of a phrase in Kathleen Norris's book *The Cloister Walk*,[49] an account of a year spent visiting a Benedictine monastery. She contrasts the call of the monks with what she observes in so many people outside the monastery who seem to be living what she refers to as 'the uncalled life', a life where there is no higher authority or purpose beyond ourselves. It is not at all that the man on the narrowboat was a bad person; it was rather that, like many people, he seemed to be living his life entirely without reference to anyone else apart from himself and, possibly, his wife. He was the centre of things, a classic 'self-made man', fulfilling Frank Sinatra's dream: 'I did it my way'. Serious discipleship is the exact opposite. It is about having *God* at the centre of our lives. This is at the heart of the promises we make in baptism. When we say 'I turn to Christ' we are making *him* the focus of our being, rather than ourselves.

To live the *called* life, to follow God and to live subject to his authority, is actually a great release from the terrible responsibility of having to decide absolutely everything for ourselves. This is not about working for the Church, being ordained or becoming a nun. It is about the focus of our being, whether we are a teacher, a banker, a cleaner at the hospital or looking after children at home.

I often watch people as they enter Ely Cathedral. It is an awe-inspiring building. The sheer size of the columns, the height of the ceiling, the uninterrupted view down the length of the nave to the great East Window. It gives people a sense of their own smallness – like looking into the Grand Canyon, standing on top of a high mountain or watching the sea crash against the rocks in a storm. It helps me to see that I am not the centre of the universe. That there are greater things than me. Perhaps, even, that there is a God in heaven. This is no bad thing. To have a right view of myself[50] is the first step on the road to humility, to which obedience is closely related.

However, it is very easy to fool ourselves. Professor John Hull tells the story of a woman he knew in Birmingham who invited her friend for lunch after church one Sunday. After lunch her friend joined her in the kitchen to do the washing up, while the husband had a sleep. After a few tentative comments about the husband's behaviour during lunch the friend said: 'Excuse me saying so, Margaret, but your husband is pissed.' Clearly shocked, Margaret replied: 'Er, I don't think so, Joyce. He's always like that.' 'Well in that case, Margaret,' insisted Joyce, 'he's always pissed!' It was the painful beginning of a realization for Margaret, and later for her husband, that he was an alcoholic. The pile of whisky bottles in the garage had not been there for years but had built up over recent weeks. The husband's funny behaviour was not because he was a bit eccentric but because he was drunk. It is so easy for us to deceive ourselves. And easy too for those closest to us to collude with that deception, out of loyalty or simply because the way we are becomes 'normal' and we can no longer see it.

Coming home on leave from Bolivia in 1983, we stayed with our friends Tom and Liz and their four children. Annie looked after the kids while I was away for much of the time speaking and preaching at churches up and down the country. It was after one such trip that I arrived home in the afternoon, tired from the journey. Annie, who was shattered from looking after sick children who were not sleeping well, asked if I wouldn't mind bathing the boys. Looking wounded, I reminded her of how hard I was working, how demanding all the speaking was, how tiring the travelling was and how I'd only just got back! So Annie went off and bathed the boys and put them to bed. Later that evening, when all the children were in bed we sat in the living room with Tom and Liz. After a while Tom looked at me and said: 'Alan, you treat your family abysmally.' It was the beginning of a serious re-evaluation of my 'work–life balance' and the painful process of change. Yet it only came about because someone whom I had known for years, who loved me and couldn't bear to see what was happening in my family, had the courage to be honest and straightforward with me. And because it was Tom, someone I knew well and trusted, I took it from him.

The first prayer in the Anglican Eucharist is a prayer against self-deception so that, as we come to worship, we might see ourselves as God sees us and worship truly, with honesty, sincerity, self-awareness and open hearts.

> Almighty God, to whom all hearts are open, all desires known, and from whom no secrets are hidden, cleanse the thoughts of our hearts by the inspiration of your Holy Spirit, that we may perfectly love you and worthily magnify your holy name, through Christ our Lord, Amen.[51]

Which is why we need to be accountable. The Iona Community, a dispersed community of lay people, takes this very seriously. All members are in 'cell groups' and are accountable to each other for their actions. They even have to account for how they spend their money, something most of us regard as private but which is actually a very major topic in the Bible, including the Gospels.[52]

For many Christians down the ages, and for a growing number today, part of that accountability can be through a 'Spiritual Director' or 'Soul Friend'. This is someone trained in listening, in spiritual guidance, in the reading of souls, someone who has insight and wisdom. Someone who can get to know us, but is sufficiently detached from our own situation not to have any personal involvement with our circle of friends and colleagues. Someone who can understand and support us but is not afraid of challenging us. Someone who can say: 'But put yourself in their shoes, Alan. How do you think you would have felt if someone had said that to you?' Or: 'Let's forget the superficial for a minute. Tell me what's really going on inside you at present.' Or: 'Don't you think you are being too hard on yourself?' Working with a Soul Friend is about building a long-term relationship of accountability, confidentiality and trust.[53]

But spiritual direction is not the only way we can be account-able. We might be part of a group of friends, where we are committed to regular meeting and to honesty and openness with one another. We might be part of a community to which we are accountable. We may have a work consultant or belong to a facilitated supervision group. Or we may have a combin-ation of these things. What is important is that we recognize our limitations, our ability to deceive ourselves, and we look for ways to become more self-aware, more open and honest before God and before one another. St John says: 'If we say we have no sin we deceive ourselves and the truth is not in us.'[54] Finding people who will help us see ourselves truly is not easy, but it is well worth the search.

I was speaking to the assistant pastor of a free church, where the pastor had just left. He was being interviewed for the job the following week and 'preaching with a view'. I asked him how he felt. 'Oh,' he said, 'we are just praying that God's will be done. I will be happy to serve whether as pastor as assistant pastor.' 'But aren't you nervous?' I asked. 'After all, there is a lot riding on this. If it were me, I would be gutted if I didn't get it. It would seem like a vote of no confidence.' Seeing there was no one around he then admitted how he was indeed nervous and really hoped he'd get the job. And he was worried how he'd manage working under someone new whom he didn't know. But he didn't feel able to express that to anyone at church, because it didn't seem very godly!

If the church wants to help us to seek the truth about God, about the world and about ourselves, it needs to be a place of honesty and openness, where we can air our doubts, fears and concerns without fear of put-down, correction or rejection.

Benedict would have us submit to authority whatever the circumstance and however unreasonable the demands made upon us. He puts great faith in a wise abbot to see that

56

authority is not abused. Personally I am not so sure. Sadly, authority is often abused. We can see this clearly in the way women have been treated down the centuries and in the frequent disclosures about children being abused by those in positions of trust and authority over them, including the Church. There is a balance to be struck between accepting authority and not allowing ourselves or others to be manipulated or even abused by its misuse. Etheldreda is, I think, a good example of someone who found herself in such a dilemma and ended up breaking her marital vows in order to follow what she perceived as a higher calling.

I remember a friend of mine, a woman curate, who was being pressured into doing something she did not think was right by one of the churchwardens. The man said to her: 'Well, you're a deacon, aren't you? I thought that meant you were called to be a servant!' 'Yes,' she replied. 'I am called to be a servant. But you are not my master.'

Being subject to authority, while not deliberately allowing ourselves to be abused by it, is a difficult balance to achieve. It is another excellent reason for finding places of 'accountability' where we can come to terms with such issues honestly and openly.

Exercise

1 Who are you accountable to for your use of time, resources and money? For your relationships, work and service? For your leisure and recreation? For how you live your life?

2 Could you identify a small group of trusted friends, with whom you might meet regularly, with whom you could be mutually accountable?

3 Have a look at the journal *Retreats*. Find a retreat house near you and, if you don't have one already, why not talk to someone

there about how you might find a Spiritual Director? If you are doing this for the first time, I suggest you agree to meet two or three times over a period of a few months, and then review how it's going. Don't get stuck with someone who is not supportive or helpful to you. On the other hand, don't end the relationship just because it's uncomfortable or challenging. That may be exactly what you need.

3

Stability

The fourth kind of monks are called gyrovagues, who spend their whole lives . . . always wandering and are never stable; slaves of self will and the attractions of gluttony; in all things they are worse than the Sarabaites.[1]

Benedict has no time for monks who wander about from one place to another. One of the Benedictine vows, along with Obedience, is 'Stability'. This essentially means that the monk vows to stay in the same monastery from his profession until his death. Even for lay people seeking to live by Benedict's Rule as oblates, this is still the case. A Benedictine 'Oblate' is attached to a single community. Thus my wife is an oblate of Turvey Abbey, but not of any other Benedictine community (unlike Franciscan Tertiaries, for example, who are not uniquely linked to a single community). For Benedict the call to discipleship means working out your salvation in the community to which you are called. If you found it not to your liking or that there was someone you really couldn't get on with, moving somewhere else was not an option.

This is completely contrary to our modern way of life, in which mobility forms a central part. I grew up in Leeds; all my extended family (about 25 of us) lived within about a mile of the centre of Leeds. We were constantly in and out of one another's houses, all within walking distance. Now none of us lives there. In any case, most of that area has been bulldozed to make way for the inner-city motorway and expansion of the universities. We are scattered to the four winds. Some moved to the surrounding commuter villages for a better life. Some went away to college or university and never came back. Some moved away because of demands of work. Some emigrated to Germany and Australia. Such mobility brings huge freedom and promotes an increasingly globalized economy. However, it comes at a price. And the price is great. As people say, you don't know what you've got until it's gone.

After my dad died, my mum became confused and increasingly dependent. We were living in Cambridge and my only brother lived in Germany. So week after week we were in the car, up the A1 to Leeds. Many of my friends recount similar stories. It was during this period that we visited our friends Eric and Adrine in Uganda. As we arrived in their home village, the truck was suddenly surrounded by people, over a hundred of them, from children to the elderly. I asked Eric: 'How many of these people are your relatives?' 'All of them,' he replied. Eric's mum, like my own, was elderly, frail and confused. However, in her case, she was surrounded by family. Caring for her personal needs, looking after her crops, doing the cooking, or just sitting, chatting to her. And it didn't all fall to a single person, as so often happens in the West, but to the whole group. She remained at the centre of the family, rather than isolated and apart from it.

A few years ago, following the tragic death of our son, Tom, from cancer, I was on the verge of being clinically depressed. I remember sitting by the front window, staring into space and thinking: 'I will never move from here, or speak to anyone, ever again.' But Michael, my golfing mate, came round to the house, or phoned me up, saying: 'Hargrave, get your butt in the car. We are playing golf.' And, together with our friend Archie, we played golf, once, twice, sometimes three times a week. We played, and I said nothing, for about six months. And then, gradually, I began to be able to express to Michael some of the pain, the desolation, the brokenness inside. Such relationships are like gold. But they do not spring up overnight. They are forged over years and they give us a clue as to how, in this highly mobile world, we might find some stability to sustain us.

There is a poignant moment in the film *Crocodile Dundee* when a transvestite at a party in New York is telling Crocodile Dundee about his relationship with his therapist. After a while Crocodile Dundee asks: 'Ain't you got any mates?' I have no wish to undermine the huge value of counselling and psychotherapy. But when we find ourselves in difficulties it is too late to think: 'Wow! I must go and get myself some mates.' We need to develop and nurture and keep those relationships going *all* the time.

Good, long-term friends are like money in the bank – except that it doesn't operate a credit system. You cannot cash in what you haven't got. Not a popular thought in a credit-dependent society. But you can't live on credit for ever, as the global banking crisis finally reminded us. It catches up with you. You set up home in a new place with new jobs. You both commute to London, earn good money and enjoy the lifestyle. Then you have your first baby. The pregnancy is difficult and leaves you exhausted. The baby, lovely as she is, isn't well and is up every night for months. You become increasingly frazzled, ratty with one another and struggling to cope. You thought you'd go back to work after three months but that doesn't seem possible at present and you start to feel the squeeze financially. Your parents live 150 miles away and so do all those mates, with whom you haven't really had time to keep up with anyway. You don't really know anybody locally and there is no one you can turn to for help. Each one of us could supply similar examples from our own experience.

How can we build stability into our lives? It doesn't look as if there will be any reverse in the trend towards globalization any time soon, so there are no painless solutions. The genie of mobility cannot be put back in the bottle. But, maybe I shouldn't go for that job in Edinburgh after all? Maybe we could downsize and live on less, so as to stay here? Perhaps we should look for the opportunity to live nearer mum and dad? It may be worth doing a bit of a relationship audit. Who are the most important people in our lives, both family and friends – the people we would turn to for help? What can we do to sustain those relationships? What do we need to do to make sure that these relationships are healthy?

A migrant worker, who had been in London for a couple of years, was interviewed before returning home to Poland. He said: 'I've had enough of doing nothing but earning money. It's more important to live among people who love you.'[2]

However, modern technology and globalization can also spring to our help. We spent ten years in South America, rarely able to phone parents, subject to the uncertainties of a rather dodgy postal system, which meant presents often went astray. Nevertheless, my mum and dad wrote to us each week, without fail, for ten years, sending little cards and notes for each of the grandchildren, never forgetting a birthday, anniversary or Christmas. Our children only saw their grandparents once every three years, but they were in no doubt that they were loved. Those relationships were like gold. Now, in that situation, the grandchildren would be on daily Skype to grandma and granddad, posting photos and videos on Facebook for each other to see. Our ability to communicate over the miles has improved dramatically.

And of course, it is not just about *me* getting support. Who are the people who look to me, depend on me, for support? Who are the people I am committed to, come what may? They may not always be people I like, but that is the nature of being committed to one another. If we are serious about discipleship we will not always have a choice about whom we live with or have responsibility for. Most of us do not get married because we fall in love with our future in-laws. But we are stuck with them nevertheless.

Abbot Christopher Jamison says in the TV programme *The Monastery*: 'The people you find most difficult are the ones who will teach you most about yourself.' How often do we hear: 'He brings out the worst in me.' Well, what is it in me that he finds so difficult and makes him react that way? Recognizing that and working with it may be more important to us than all the easy times we spend with those we get on with. Getting married is 'for better, for worse'. The times that are 'for better' can be wonderful. But it is how we handle the 'for worse' times that will determine our future together. Brother Roger tells us: 'Perfection is precisely to suffer one's neighbour's imperfections, and to do so out of love.'[3]

The 'for worse' times are not just when we have a major disagreement to cope with. They are often when we are just fed up, bored with each other and stop communicating. It can be even more difficult when a relationship is uneven, when we cannot expect or do not receive in proportion to how much we are called upon to give. When the other person is no longer able to reciprocate or repay. When the other has a long-term illness or depression. When our painful experience is: 'It's all one way.' Yet this too is part of our commitment to one another. My mum needed us a lot after my dad died. But then I think of all the many, many years of mum and dad's generous, wholehearted, selfless love towards us. As W. H. Auden puts it:

> If equal affection cannot be
> Let the more loving one be me.[4]

Turning the other cheek, going the extra mile, offering hospitality to the people who cannot repay. These are core gospel values, without which our communities and churches would rapidly become 'PLUs' – people like us – instead of embracing everyone in lasting relationships of committed love and support.

Faithfulness

Stability is not unrelated to faithfulness. The words 'faith' or 'belief' have, for many of us, the connotation of affirming a series of propositions about God. Thus we express our faith by saying one of the creeds, a doctrinal statement about the Trinity. However, biblically, 'faith' has much more to do with 'faithfulness' than with intellectual assent or certainty. This is intimately linked to how we live our lives. If we read the letters of St Paul alongside the epistle of St James we see different emphases on faith. However, the common factor is that genuine 'faith' involves integrity of inner conviction with the way we live.

Throughout the Old Testament God's covenant with his people is about faithfulness. Even when his people are unfaithful (which is generally the case) God remains faithful. This is captured by the enigmatic saying recorded in the second letter to Timothy:

If we are faithless, God remains faithful,
for he cannot deny himself.[5]

Faithfulness is also what we promise in our marriage vows:

For better, for worse,
for richer, for poorer,
in sickness and in health,
to love and to cherish,
till death us do part.[6]

The implication is that we stick with it, when things are going well and everything is hunky-dory; and especially when they aren't, when the wheels have come off and we are sick of the sight of each other. The romantic idea of love will not be sufficient to steer us through such rocky times. I stayed with a Hindu couple and their two teenage children in Luton some years ago. The couple obviously enjoyed a close, loving relationship, even though their marriage had been arranged. I asked the wife, one day, if she had loved her husband when they got married. 'Oh no,' she replied. 'I did not get married *because* I loved my husband. I got married *in order to* love my husband.'

So it is with our commitment to community, to relationships in general. C. S. Lewis says: 'Do not waste time bothering whether you "love" your neighbour. Act as if you did. When you behave as if you loved someone, you will presently come to love him. If you injure someone you dislike you will find yourself disliking him more. If you do him a good turn you will find yourself disliking him less.'[7]

Faithfulness is easy when we are getting on well with people; when life at home is a joy and our parents are in rude health, living round the corner; when our friends are supportive but not demanding; when our church life is flourishing and our career blossoming. But when relationships are difficult; when our friends are going through a painful time and are leaning on us more than we can bear; when our marriage is rocky and the kids are a pain; when our parents are confused, increasingly dependent and live 200 miles away; when church is boring; when the new neighbours play music till 2 a.m. and never mow the grass; when the job is going badly but there is a great one advertised in France – that's when our call to stability and faithfulness is really tested. That's when the temptation to cut and run kicks in and we dream about a fresh start. Which is not to say that moving away is never the right thing to do.

Rather, the call to faithfulness should make us examine most carefully our motives and our commitments and make us wonder if this isn't simply the 'for worse' through which we have to struggle, or to use St Paul's words, to 'work out your salvation'.[8] This comes, of course, in the context of his description of Christ giving up the riches of heaven, to humble himself as a servant, even to the point of his death on the cross. Faithfulness, and hence stability, comes at a price. But, argues Paul, a price well worth paying.

Of course, giving up the riches of heaven to become a human being means, in practice, God in Christ limiting himself to a single body, with all its limitations. It means not doing some things in order to do others better. Part of my problem is trying to cram too much in – until something has to give. Like my Christmas tree.

On my way back home I notice a sign that says: 'Christmas trees. Cut your own. £10 or £15.' I pull in and talk to the assistant, a lad of about 17. He takes me down to where the trees are growing. I choose a large one, the non-drop type. If my wife had been here she'd have suggested one about a quarter the size. But she isn't. So I choose a big one. The chain-saw isn't working so the assistant saws it down by hand. It takes a while. Finally we get it back to the car. 'How much?' I ask. 'Fifteen quid,' he replies. Pretty good for a 10-ft tree! I am so pleased I give him an extra fiver as a tip. I open the boot of the Fiat Panda hatchback and shove the tree in, trunk first. Unfortunately the tree is too long. Perhaps I should have thought about the size of the car first? Too late now. We cut off a couple of feet but it's still too long – but only by an inch or two. If I slam the boot it will probably just sort itself out and fit in. I slam the boot. There is a sickening, cracking noise as the foot of the tree goes through the windscreen. Turns out to be a pretty expensive tree. £15 for the tree. £5 tip. £75 insurance waiver for a new windscreen. Not to mention the personal cost of having to confess to my wife.

It's the old problem. Trying to fit too much in and getting myself into a mess. Faithfulness means having the space to fit in the people I'm committed to and not just see them as a tremendous inconvenience in their hour of need.

Exercise

10 times.

1 How many times have you moved house in the past 20 years? What were your reasons for moving? What might make you move again? What alternatives are there to moving?

2 What are the really important, long-term relationships in your life? Whom do you look to for support, friendship, advice? What can you do to nourish and sustain these relationships so that they will grow and develop over the next 10, 20, 50 years?

Keep being

my children

3 Who are the key people who look to you for support and care – the family, friends, colleagues, others – whom you know you need to be committed to long term? What can you do to sustain those relationships and make sure you are there for them when they need you? How might you work with others to make sure the burden of care does not just fall to one or two people?

4 What communities sustain, support and challenge you? Are there people who are no longer able to be part of these communities, perhaps due to failing health or personal circumstances? How can you, as a community, continue to support them?

5 What experience do you have of people sticking with you through difficult times, even when it cost them? Have you felt 'dropped' by people you hoped would support you in your hour of need? What can you learn from those experiences?

long-term friends

6 Are you overstretched, not doing anything well? What might you give up in order to do the core things better? How might you withdraw from some things which are not sustainable without leaving others in the lurch?

No

Have to keep a balance of activity with slow legs —

4

Work

—◆●◆—

For your prayer to be real, you must get to grips with hard
work . . . Your prayer will become total when it is one with your
work.[1]

As we have already noted, for Benedict the most important
work is the '*Opus Dei*', the work we offer God in our prayers,
worship and study. And that *is* work – it does not come easily
or naturally to the majority of us. Certainly not to me.

However, for most of us, what we consider our 'work' will
be that which employs much of our time and pays the bills.
It always saddens me when I ask people what they do and
they reply: 'nothing'. What they often mean is they work 24/7
looking after an elderly parent or two lively children (or sometimes both)! So much of the value we attach to work is about
remuneration. Yet much of the most important work may be
poorly paid or often unpaid.

Take 'Aunty Brenda', for example, my mum's next-door
neighbour of 30 years. Her husband was a skilled craftsman
but, since having children, she has never been 'out to work'. Yet
for years she ran the voluntary community-care group in the
village, looking after the needs of many elderly, chronically sick,
lonely and housebound people. Thus when my mum developed
dementia, after my dad died, Brenda would go round four, five
or even six times a day to see my mum. She sat and chatted
with her. Did her shopping. Got her prescriptions. Sorted out

69

her tablets. Did the washing. Cleaned up the mess. Latterly she cooked all mum's meals, never wanting a penny in return, telling us instead how much she loved my mum and how much my mum and dad had done for her, when her kids were little. And my mum wasn't the only one she cared for, cycling around the village with freshly baked scones. Yet talking to Brenda, and hearing her make light of her own remarkable contribution to the community life of the village, including her life-giving support to my mum, you would imagine she sat in front of the TV all day, doing nothing.

Many of us today tend to think of work as a creative, purpose-filled activity, something we choose and something we may decide to change, if it does not provide the satisfaction or remuneration we had hoped for. However, in much of the world, and until very recent times in the West, apart from a tiny, wealthy minority, work does not involve any choice. It is often back-breaking, repetitive, tiresome, and yet absolutely necessary to sustain daily life.

Benedict's Rule reflects this. All are to be engaged in some sort of manual labour as well as in study. Benedict, like St Paul, has no time for idleness.[2] No difference is made between those who are of noble birth and those from a poor background. However, compassion is shown to those who are unwell or unable to work and people's special skills are recognized and used, providing they do not thereby abuse their position. Underlying all this is the most important concept of all: that our work is *service*, working for the benefit of others.

This is in sharp contrast to how we often perceive of work in our society, as essentially for our own benefit. We speak of being 'self-made' men or women; of deserving the benefits we enjoy through our hard work. Yet the language of discipleship, not just for monks but for all of us, reminds us that everything we have comes from God, including our abilities, creativity and energy. But for God's grace we might have been born into a refugee family in Darfur. But for God's grace we may have been brought up in the inner city with no dad and a mum who is an alcoholic. But for God's grace we might have been born with severe learning disabilities. We can choose to use our skills and our resources essentially for ourselves. Or we can see them as gifts to be shared and use them for the common good. Our attitude, Jesus tells us, should be that of humble servants: 'So, when you have done everything you were ordered to do say, "We are worthless slaves, we have only done what we ought to have done." '³ If this sounds rather harsh, it is said as a deliberate warning to us about the cost of offering everything we have, and everything we are, in God's service. After all, as the offertory prayer in the communion service reminds us:

All things come from you, and of your own do we give you.⁴

There is a great paradox here. Jesus tells us that whoever wishes to save their life will lose it and whoever loses their life for the sake of the gospel will save it.⁵ This is not just a reference to some future state in heaven. He is speaking of the reality of our experience now. Offering both our work and the material benefits it brings as service to others transforms our own lives, as well as the lives of those whom we serve.

Work/work balance

Work/life balance is a popular theme, the subject of many books. But work/work balance deserves some consideration too. Like many people I know, I tend to overwork. I sometimes wonder why this is? I get paid the same if I work 30 hours per week or 70. Indeed, the less I work, the greater the hourly rate! So why bother with the extra hours? For me the answer, in part at least, lies in the type of work I do. My work is varied, but there are some things I *have* to do: there are particular meetings and worship services I need to attend; there is administrative stuff that just has to be dealt with; there are the dreaded emails. I have to do all these core tasks before I can get on with the interesting, creative stuff that I really enjoy doing. This is true both of my paid work and of the jobs I do around the house or in a voluntary capacity. So, I end up overworking because I take on too many interesting and exciting things that I cannot bear to let go of.

Having balance in our work is important. I know people who have particular things they love doing at work, things they leave until they've done something boring, as a kind of personal reward: 'deferred gratification'. For me, I often find myself doing anything, even the washing up, rather than getting down to the job I really don't want to do. Yet if we see our work as service there are some things connected with this that are of great importance.

To begin with, how does the way I work relate to others? If I am called to service then I am called to make sure, in as much as it depends on me, that I am not the only one doing the enjoyable and rewarding jobs. In my previous post I had a lot of 'ordinands' (trainee vicars) on placement. I had to discipline myself to give them some of the really interesting people to visit, not just the ones I didn't want to go and see. And to let them have a go at the school assembly, even though I knew I would probably do a better job myself. Otherwise how were they ever to learn and to develop their own skills? And it also means, in practice, that I sometimes have to pick up the 'donkey work' so others can go to the conference, design the poster or attend the lunch.

It is also very easy, if we are competent at what we do, to 'de-skill' others, particularly if we work in an area where people do not have high self-esteem. When we needed help with our children's work on a council estate, I wondered about asking an ordinand to take it on. After all, they had the skills and I was pretty sure they'd do a good job. But how would that help develop the leadership of the church in the long term? Having thought about it, I asked, instead, our church cleaner, a young woman, a single parent, if she'd like to help with the Sunday Club. 'Oh no,' she replied. 'I'm useless. Thick as two short planks. Rubbish. I couldn't do that. No way!' I finally persuaded her to have a go, at least as an assistant. After a few weeks the person leading Sunday Club became ill and had to give it up, so Tracey took over. She turned out to be brilliant! Enthusiastic, creative, committed. I went into the Sunday Club room after church one day to discover the whole place turned into the belly of a whale. The door had become huge jaws through which you had to enter. The room was in darkness, paper intestines hanging from the ceiling. She was helping the children think about the story of Jonah. And, in the dark 'belly of the whale', she helped the kids to talk about their experiences of dark and difficult times.

Over the following two years she started doing a couple of A levels at night-school and then applied to do a Youth Work degree. She began to run a youth group and recruited kids from the street who'd never been near church before. It was tough going – financially, emotionally and in every way – both for her and for those who supported her. She was 'in your face', volatile, moody. Yet she ended up with a 2.1 honours degree and the best mark in her final dissertation of anyone doing the course! *formal speech on essay*

I think of another single parent in her 40s, a cleaner, who dropped out of education in her teens. Encouraged by her boss to think about studying, she has just completed the first stage of an NVQ. 'This is the first certificate I have ever had in my whole life,' she said, her face beaming with pride.

Our work is not just about fulfilling our *own* potential, but enabling others to fulfil theirs as well. And that includes those (perhaps especially those) who would lack the self-worth and confidence to realize their own potential without the ongoing encouragement and support of the rest of us.

When people tell John the Baptist that some of his followers are leaving him in order to follow Jesus, instead of feeling irritated or threatened, he is delighted. 'My joy is now complete,' he replies. 'He must increase, I must decrease.'[6] Like John, we need to keep reminding ourselves why we are here. It is not about my fantasy of becoming rich and famous! It is to let others flourish, so they can fulfil all the potential that God has put within them. And in allowing others to flourish, we often find true freedom and fulfilment ourselves. 'You fear a common rule may stifle your personality,' says Brother Roger, 'whereas its purpose is to free you from useless shackles.'[7]

And here is another important principle. If work is service, then nothing must be beneath me. Sometimes it will have to be me who does the jobs no one wants to do: me who mops up the toilet; me who clears up after the meeting. It is amazing how many men turn out to be 'no good' at changing nappies. 'It makes me feel sick,' they moan. Well, I dare say it makes many mothers feel sick, too. So, get over it and start changing.

Humble service is important because it keeps us rooted in who we are before God. On the night before he dies, Jesus does not take the best place at table and wait to be served. Instead, he takes a bowl of water and a towel and washes the disciples' feet, filthy from walking the dirt roads in open sandals.[8]

Exercise

1 What do you really hate about your job? What is really fulfilling and enjoyable?

2 What might you be able to do to help make the work of your colleagues more fulfilling, even if it means your giving up some of the stuff you enjoy?

3 What gifts do you have that you are not really using at present? How might you begin to express them?

4 Who are the people in your workplace/community who do not have the confidence or self-esteem to express the gifts within them? What might you do, as a community, to help them realize their potential?

Humility

Humility is at the heart of discipleship. The word is derived from the Latin '*humus*' meaning earth. Humility 'suggests that we should be profoundly earthed, that we should face up to the truth about our human condition'.[9] Having a right view of ourselves in the light of who God is. Benedict devotes his longest chapter to humility and offers us a twelve-step stairway to measure our progress.[10] These steps are worthy of serious consideration, though they may sound rather painful and difficult for us today. And they are deeply rooted in Scripture.

We live in a society where, for many, the highest goal in life seems to be to appear on TV, to be famous, to become a celebrity. Oscar Wilde famously said: 'There is only one thing in the world worse than being talked about and that is not being talked about.' Humility removes from us the insidious need to be forever comparing ourselves with others, trying to get ourselves noticed, thinking about the next career move rather than what we are actually called to be now. True humility implies contentment, not in the sense of lacking ambition or failing to use our talents to the full, but in the sense of being able to live and enjoy the moment, rather than always looking to the next main chance.

Mario, Anglican Bishop in northern Argentina and a Native American, came to stay with us on his way back from a trip to the UK some years ago. He had never left South America before and he spoke no English. He showed us his photos. 'This is Michael and Virginia. Here's one of me with Kevin and Denise and their boys. This is Pat and Val. And here's one of me and Robert.' The one of 'me and Robert' was, in fact, a photo of Mario with Archbishop Robert Runcie, inside Lambeth Palace. But for Mario he was just another of the friends he had made on his trip to England.

What a blessed release, not to have to impress anybody with my name-dropping. What freedom, to be able to treat every person the same, regardless of their status. And what a contrast to my own life! Hoping the Dean has sufficiently appreciated how much effort I put into the Vision Document. Wondering who is taking note of my speech at General Synod. Getting noticed at that Cathedrals' conference. The truth is that I am full of mixed motives. I want to love God for his own sake and to love and serve my neighbours, whoever they are, without partiality. But I also want to be popular, well thought of, fulfilled, successful – whatever that means! I want to use my God-given talents to the full. But I also want recognition and promotion. How very difficult true humility is.

Some time ago I applied for a job that I thought I'd be good at and had a pretty good chance of getting. In fact, I wasn't even short-listed. I was gutted. I mentioned it to my friend Michael, while we were playing golf. He paused for a moment, hit a magnificent drive down the middle of the fairway, and said: 'The thing is this, Alan. God calls us to be humble. But we're not. So he has to humble us instead. Which he does.' I stepped up to the tee and hooked my drive straight into the pond. I have a long way to go, and not just in golf, either.

Read more — Books about the saints

Exercise

1 What are your goals, ambitions for the future? Why are they important to you? What are your motives in pursuing them? How do they fit with the goals, ambitions of those you love, those you work with, those you are committed to? Whom can you have an honest conversation with about this?

2 Go carefully through Benedict's Twelve Steps to Humility.[11] Rewrite each one in a single sentence, as you think it applies to you yourself. Pin up the summary somewhere you will see it – your office, the loo, the kitchen noticeboard – and think about it regularly. You may wish to do this as a group and share your list with others.

Simplicity

Your availability calls for continual simplification of your existence.

The boldness to use, in the best way possible, all present day goods, without fearing possible poverty, to lay up no capital, gives incalculable strength.[12]

Cathy was a staunch Methodist all her life, a woman of strong opinions, a character. In her 80s and disabled, she spent her days in the back, downstairs room of her small council house, reading her Bible, sitting in front of a paraffin stove so as not to waste money on expensive central heating. On the wall was a photo of me with the Methodist minister – or rather, a photo of our legs! 'I can't help fancying legs,' she'd say, with a chuckle. Whenever I went to visit her she would hand me a grubby envelope stuffed with £10 notes. 'This is for the pipeline,' she'd whisper. 'Let not the right hand know what the left hand doeth,'[13] meaning 'Don't tell anybody.' The pipeline was a water project we supported in Uganda. Over a two-year period she gave me

Mat. 6: 3–4

amazing

over £1000 for the 'pipeline', which she had saved out of her state pension and benefits.

Coupled with humility is the concept of simplicity. Consumerism is the very antithesis of monastic life. It threatens our inner, spiritual life more than we might imagine. It also threatens the earth's limited resources. How we use those resources needs to begin with understanding ourselves in relation to creation. If we think of ourselves as owners, we will claim the right to use the resources at our disposal as we see fit, regardless of the impact on the planet. If we think of ourselves as individuals we will not worry too much what impact our use of resources has on anyone else. However, if we see ourselves as created beings, called to be stewards of that which is not ultimately ours, but God's, then we are accountable for everything about the way we live our lives, for our impact on others and on the global environment.[14] If we see ourselves as part of humanity, how can we ever be truly content while others suffer want? As John Donne famously said:

> No man is an island, entire of itself . . . Any man's death dimin-
> ishes me because I am involved in mankind. And therefore never
> send to know for whom the bell tolls; it tolls for thee.[15]

Even secular organizations such as Greenpeace and Oxfam know this. They have pioneered care for the environment and justice for the poor. The Church has not always been first to promote such causes.

Yet it is not just concern for people and the environment that should make us think about Simplicity. The more our energies and attention are taken up by the cares of property and possessions, by the demands of fashion, by the allure of the adverts, the less freedom we have to 'live well'. Paradoxically we live in a society that not only has the greatest prosperity ever but also the greatest degree of dissatisfaction. The Australian cartoonist Michael Leunig offers us this prayer:

> God help us. With great skill and energy we have ignored the state of the human heart. With politics and economics we have ignored the heart's needs. With eloquence, wit and reason we have belittled the heart's wisdom. With sophistication and style, with science and technology, we have drowned out the voice of the soul. We cannot hear the heart's truth and thus we have betrayed and belittled ourselves and pledged madness to our children. With skill and pride we have made for ourselves an unhappy society.[16]

For Benedict's monks, stewardship involved control of diet, of clothing, of living accommodation, of resources. They were given a sufficient allowance – ample by the standards of their day. Yet they held no 'private' property, and any form of greed or holding of personal possessions was dealt with most severely. This gave them tremendous freedom, following Christ's own exhortation not to be anxious about any of these things.[17] It also meant that they always had the resources to welcome guests and to support the poor. Benedict reminds the brethren that 'guests are to be welcomed as Christ, for he is going to say: "I was a stranger and you welcomed me",'[18] and 'special care is to be shown in the reception of the poor and of pilgrims, for in them especially is Christ received'.[19]

There could hardly be a greater contrast between the simplicity of the monastery and my own life. In 1984 we moved from La Paz, Bolivia's capital city, high in the Altiplano, to Santa Cruz, 500 miles away in the lowlands. We rented a house and moved in, waiting for our goods to arrive by truck, a two-day overland journey. In the meantime we survived on some borrowed mattresses, a few chairs, a table, some crockery, cutlery and pans. After five days the truck had still not arrived. We rang the company in La Paz and were assured it had left on time. A week passed; ten days. We were beginning to think that the truck must have had an accident, gone over a cliff on the winding mountain roads or been attacked by robbers. We became increasingly anxious about the welfare of all the things we'd accumulated over the years. But we were also getting used to living with less, and it was OK. Resigned to the loss, we were astonished at how well we managed without a lot of stuff we hardly ever used and, probably, didn't need. Then one day, after two and a half weeks, without any warning, the truck turned up, with all our goods intact. 'Well,' explained the driver, in a quite unapologetic way, 'there was a family wedding in Cochabamba on the way, so what could I do? I could hardly not stay for it, now could I?' They began to unload. I was amazed at how much stuff we had. Our maid, Marcie, kept saying: 'Gosh, what a lot of crockery you've got! Wow! What a lot of cutlery! Goodness me, look at all that bedding and furniture! Haven't you got a lot of clothes!? And just look at all these books!' For the first time in my life I began to feel ashamed and to realize what a huge amount of unnecessary stuff we'd accumulated. Yet now, living in a very large house at the side of Ely Cathedral, we have accumulated even more.

And our accumulation is not just an individual matter. Our personal choices about using the earth's resources and spending on ourselves is a small, but significant, component of what happens in the world at large.

A couple of years ago we went on holiday to Northumberland. On our trip to the Farne Islands we were sad to learn that there were fewer puffins nesting than usual and fewer chicks surviving. 'Not enough for them to eat,' we were told. 'The sea has become too warm for the sand eels on which they feed their young.' We see another example of changing climate on the Fens where we live. Little egrets, once a rare visitor to our shores, are now found in breeding colonies here as the climate warms.[20]

These are small examples which remind us that we stand on the brink of irreversible damage to the earth. We can no longer claim that we do not know about global warming, the depletion of the earth's limited resources or the exploitation of cheap or forced labour to produce the items we buy daily. We cannot but face our calling to be good stewards.

In answer to the commandment to 'love your neighbour as yourself' a lawyer asks Jesus, 'Who is my neighbour?'[21] But Jesus turns the question around and asks instead: 'Who is the neighbour to the one who is in need?' These days we see our neighbours portrayed daily on our TV and computer screens. We see our neighbours in Kenya and Colombia asking if we care about them enough to ensure they get a decent price for the coffee and tea they produce. We see our neighbours in Bangladesh, asking us how much more the sea level will rise as a result of our energy use. We see our neighbours in sweatshops in India and China wondering why we don't pay more for our clothes so they can earn a living wage. We see our neighbours in refugee camps in Darfur asking if we have any spare cash to help buy tents and urgent medical supplies. It means saying 'no' to more for ourselves. It means that enough has, indeed, to be enough.

Yet there are the beginnings of a disillusionment with our materialistic, hedonistic society. For example: 'Stop reading women's magazines! They are the devil's own work.' This is advice *not* from a fundamentalist religious sect but from Oliver James's secular best-seller![22] This is not just about altruism. It is about finding a life which is deeply satisfying for ourselves. The keys to simplicity are Gratitude, Generosity and Contentment.[23] To be thankful for what we have and to see it as God's gift to us, rather than a reward for our labours. To use it generously in God's service, for the benefit of all, not just ourselves. And to learn to be content with what we have, rather than always looking to have the next new thing. This is not easy for us. It involves a constant spiritual battle with ourselves and within our families and church communities. It involves living differently. We might ask ourselves, as Christians: 'If we were to line up alongside those who don't go to church, what would it be about our lifestyle that makes us different?' I think of local campaigns on behalf of Fairtrade, Amnesty and other issues. I might feel pleased that we are a Fairtrade Cathedral and Diocese. But why is it that Wales, for example, became a Fairtrade nation long before we got the message?

Bishop Mario recounted a visit to a particularly poor area of northern Argentina, on the frontier of Bolivia and Paraguay. He commented on how poor the people of a particular village were, and yet how happy they seemed. He suggested starting a development project to help them economically. The people listened quietly. Then, one of the elders replied: 'We thank you, Bishop, for your concern. However, people regularly come through our village and say they want to help us – government officials, Church leaders, important organizations from across the world. They say: "Oh! Your situation is so terrible. We must start a project to help you." But, frankly, nothing much ever seems to happen. We are poor. We were born poor and we will die poor. However, that is only on the outside. Inside we are very rich, for we know the love of Christ, deep within us.'

Desmond Tutu recounts the story of standing alongside a man whose family home, everything they owned, was being flattened by one of the apartheid regime's bulldozers. The Archbishop suggested they pray, but he was so shocked and appalled he couldn't find any words to say. After a while the man himself prayed. 'Dear God, we thank you that you love us.'[24]

The seventeenth-century poet George Herbert says:

Thou that hast giv'n so much to me
Give one thing more, a gratefull heart . . .

Not thankfull when it pleaseth me;
As if thy blessings had spare days;
But such a heart whose pulse may be
Thy Praise.[25]

Exercise

Why not try this exercise with a group of friends and then talk about it together:

Simplicity. Think of one *significant* thing you'd *really* like – but don't actually need. Something you'd planned to do or to buy. Then, decide *not* to do it or to buy it.

Generosity. However much you'd planned to spend on that thing you were going to do or to buy – give the equivalent amount of money away to the charity of your choice instead. As you give it, try and think yourself into the lives of the people your giving is supporting.

Gratitude. Instead of focusing on the thing you wanted but haven't bought, make a daily, conscious effort to think about and thank God for what you *have* got. And take the opportunity warmly to thank others as well for what they contribute to your well-being.

Contentment. Try to develop the habit of living more in the present, rather than always thinking about the future. How about completely avoiding the Argos catalogue, IKEA, Next, *your* M&S, the jobs pages, the *Good Food Guide*, *Hello!* magazine, *X Factor*, the Lottery, eBay, bargainholidays.com (or whatever your particular temptation is) for a few weeks?

Hospitality

It is Christ himself whom we receive in a guest. So let us learn to welcome.[26]

An essential part of the work of the monastery is to offer hospitality. This takes the form both of providing a place to stay for visitors but also providing food for the poor. This is quite unlike the culture of inviting family, mates or work colleagues round for a meal. This is offering hospitality to strangers and to those who cannot repay the favour.

We arrive in the village of Santa Maria in northern Argentina on a hot, sticky evening after a difficult journey across dirt roads. It is my first trip into the heart of the Chaco. It is a journey that normally takes four hours but in fact took us two days. When we set off the truck was empty apart from me and Annette, my senior colleague, in the cab. However, after visiting a couple of villages and attending to the queues of people wanting lifts, I found myself perched precariously on top of the huge pile of bags on the back of the truck. I had commented to Annette that it looked as if we were in for rain and wouldn't it be worth getting some mud tyres? 'Have faith, brother,' she replies, as she presses on regardless. By the middle of the night, in pouring rain, with the truck sliding around in the mud, my faith is at a very low ebb. I find myself muttering darkly about how it is OK for Annette to have faith. She is clean and dry inside the truck. Unlike the rest of us! I manage to dig a pair of wellies out of the back of the truck and put them on, in the dark. We then push the truck for several hours, through the night, until we slide off the road into a deep ditch and are unable to move. My feet are killing me. As the dawn breaks I wash the mud off the boots in a nearby puddle, to discover that I have the boots on the wrong feet. Finally, we struggle into the

Has a good sense of humour

village, late the following day. I feel desolate – hungry, angry, wet, exhausted and nursing blisters on both feet. Yet, as we arrive, people begin to emerge from their mud huts to meet us. They surround the truck and greet us with smiling faces and warm hugs. They prepare a house for us to sleep in and cook a huge banquet of freshly caught fish. They stand around, laughing and chatting, as they watch us eat their precious fish, not eating themselves. I have never been here nor ever met any of these people before, but they receive me like a long-lost son. They have given us enough food to feed a large family for a week, though they themselves are desperately poor.

We have received many great acts of generous hospitality. Friends and family, for example, who opened their homes for us to stay, for months at a time, when we were on leave in the UK from South America. Yet perhaps the greatest acts of generosity have come from very poor people. It is often the case that, the better off we become, the more protective we are of our possessions and the more suspicious of others. Can you imagine turning up unknown and unannounced in an English suburb, late one evening, and having the whole street turn out to welcome you, offer you accommodation, and cooking you a celebration meal? Even if they knew you well, they might not be too keen to get out of bed at 2 a.m., cook you a meal and give up their own bedroom, just for you.

> When you give a dinner party, do not invite your friends, or brothers or relatives or rich neighbours, lest they invite you back and you are repaid. Instead invite the poor, the crippled, the lame and the blind and you will be blessed, for they cannot repay but you will be repaid at the resurrection of the righteous.[27]

Such hospitality has become even more important in our day because of increased globalization. We travel across the world but the world is also living on our doorstep, often uneasily.

opening the door to strangers.

Ethnic and religious conflicts are evident everywhere we look. We hear people speak about the need for tolerance. However, tolerance, though important, is not enough. Tolerance is a passive quality. It often means grudgingly bearing that which we do not like. I can tolerate someone or put up with their behaviour without making any effort to welcome, know or understand them – or indeed to receive the hospitality they might offer me, if I bothered to approach them. As we have seen, Christ asks of us not tolerance, but generous hospitality, the opening of our hearts to the other, especially to the stranger.

Of course, such hospitality is costly, risky even, which is why we tend to avoid it. The Northumbria Community Rule of 'availability' and 'vulnerability' reflects this. If we make ourselves available, we become vulnerable. We were asked, some years ago, to put up a young man, arriving from La Paz to Santa Cruz, for a week or two 'until he found his feet'. He stayed for two years. If we take hospitality seriously we run the risk of being taken advantage of, suffering loss. But perhaps an even greater risk is that of missing out on meeting Christ, unawares.

One of the most hopeful events of 2007, barely mentioned in the news, was an open letter from 138 prominent Muslim scholars representing every shade of Islam, to Christian and political leaders in the West.[28] It is called 'A Common Word between Us and You'. It is an invitation to join an ongoing dialogue based upon the call to love our neighbour and to offer hospitality, found in both the Bible and the Qur'an. Indeed, this tradition of hospitality to the stranger, to people outside our own community, is central to all major faiths. It includes not just a duty to offer hospitality to strangers, but the idea that God may meet us in the stranger, that we might be entertaining angels unawares.[29] Yet there are also strands in all our faiths

Hebrews 13:

of exclusivity, of keeping out those who do not conform to our ideas or ways of living. For example, many Anglicans from the Afro-Caribbean communities, who came here after the war, were made to feel so unwelcome that they ended up founding their own churches, where they could belong. Part of our unwillingness to engage is our fear of difference, of change, of the perceived threat to our own identity, and our desire for self-protection. Yet it is often through such risky encounters that we meet God and are ourselves changed. D. H. Lawrence, reflecting on Abraham's meeting with the three strange visitors by the Oaks of Mamre,[30] expresses this conflict within us:

> What is the knocking?
> What is the knocking at the door in the night?
> It is somebody wants to do us harm.
> No, no, it is the three strange angels.
> Admit them. Admit them.[31]

Best of the book

As we look around us, there are an awful lot of people waiting to be let in. It may be children dying of Aids in Africa, the Palestinians in Gaza, people flooded in Mozambique, the homeless people on our doorstep, or the unvisited, elderly down our street. Leviticus 19 contains those famous words, quoted by Jesus: 'You shall love your neighbour as yourself.' Less well-known, in that same chapter, is the exhortation: 'When a foreigner resides with you in your land, you shall not oppress the foreigner. He shall be to you as a citizen. *You shall love the foreigner as yourself* because you too were once foreigners in Egypt.'[32] *Leviticus*

Working for the 'Common Good', as opposed to working simply for our own good, is a concept desperately needed in our own communities, in society around us and across the world. It is a deeply Christian concept which has at its heart loving our neighbour as ourselves.[33] It reflects a God who does not keep himself to himself in heaven, but comes down, to share our humanity, to enter deeply into our lives, accepting our hospitality and offering us his astonishing love and blessing in return.

And it is as we offer generous hospitality that God is seen in us. This is not about having ulterior motives for welcoming people, but about recognizing what a profound impact such encounters can have. Furthermore, the quality of our own inner life will be of huge importance in such encounters. Rowan Williams says: 'The saint isn't someone who makes you think: "That looks hard . . . that's too hard for me" but someone who makes us think: "How astonishing (that) human lives can be like that . . . How can I find what they have found?"'[34] Whatever people's response, generous hospitality is part of our discovery of Christ, who tells us: 'Whatever you did to the least of these, you did it to me.'[35] *mattheo 25 : 31*

Exercise

1 Who are the people you come into contact with who are strangers or foreigners? How might you take the initiative in making them welcome, offering hospitality?

Rented houses in Amey)

2 Can you think of a time when you were offered generous hospitality from an unexpected source? What was your reaction to it?

Rest and recreation

When we lived in Santa Cruz, in Bolivia, one of our American friends told us of his despair at the local people, many of whom seemed to do the minimum amount of work in order to spend as much time as possible sitting under a tree, with their family and friends, talking, playing the guitar, singing, playing with the kids, drinking beer. 'If they worked a bit harder', he'd say, 'they could provide a better life for themselves and their family.' However, the truth was that, despite material poverty, they had a very rich family life, spending far more time with one another than many of us in the West, who commute for hours and burn the midnight oil in a demanding career which leaves little time for our loved ones. The people in Santa Cruz were not working for an imagined future. They were living now. They did not live for their work, as many of us do. They worked in order to live. They perhaps have a lot to teach us about 'getting a life'.

I often hear myself and others complain of being overworked, of the many demands upon us. However, it is hard to think of anyone more in demand than Jesus. He was mobbed by the crowds wherever he went. He had to get up before dawn to find any time to be on his own. Yet he did not simply work 24/7 to get through all the people on the waiting list. He had clear priorities.[36] He also knew that he and his disciples needed Rest and Recreation – 'R and R'. He says to his disciples: '"Come with me to a quiet place all by yourselves and rest for a while", for so many people were coming and going that they had no chance even to eat.'[37] Of course, it didn't always quite work out that way, as on this occasion, where they are spotted by the crowd, who follow them to the other side of the lake. Nevertheless, we clearly see Jesus, again and again, taking not just time to rest and pray, but time to enjoy life and relax. Indeed, it is one of the Pharisees' criticisms of him: 'Look, a glutton and a drunkard!'[38] He even turns up at a wedding banquet in Cana at the beginning of his ministry and produces an extra 600 litres of top-quality wine, when the wedding guests are already drunk – not, perhaps, a practice we would want to encourage![39]

What we see in Jesus is God limited by humanity. He only has one body. He cannot be in more than one place at once.

He cannot do everything. Some people are disappointed.[40] Like Jesus before us we are limited human beings, needing to take time out if we are to get a right balance in our lives and sustain any sort of long-term vocation.

I sometimes find it depressing talking to busy professional people or clergy colleagues about 'R and R'. Many of them always seem to be *about to go* to the gym, or *about to start* that hobby, or *about to go* swimming with the kids. My friend regularly played golf with his grandchildren. He lamented the fact that though their dad played golf as well, he almost never had time to play with his boys. 'One of these days', he said, 'he'll want to play with them, but it will be too late.' A lot of us just need to 'get a life', to discover the Mars Bar balance of 'work, rest and play'.[41]

Even in the monastery, Benedict assigns time for rest.[42] Rest is all the more enjoyable and refreshing when it comes in the context of work. We not only feel the need for rest but appreciate it more. The film *Into Great Silence* portrays the lives of the Carthusian monks of Grande Chartreuse, a strict, silent order situated in the French Alps. Infrequently, the monks are allowed to walk and talk together. On one such occasion we see them sliding down the snow slopes, falling over, laughing and joking together, thoroughly enjoying this rare opportunity. The rarity of opportunity seems to enhance the flavour of the moment. It is as though their silence has made them acutely appreciative of the beauty and great value of the world and of one another.

Which brings us back to Benedict's appeal for balance – in this case a right balance between work and leisure, between going off to a 'quiet place' and having a party, between being on our own and relaxing with others. After all, if even God needs a rest, then so do we.[43] Genesis 2

Of course, a day a week off is not possible for everyone. International aid workers stuck in a refugee camp, for example, find it pointless to try and have a day off there. They might, however, take a week off in a different location, after a six-week spell of duty. There is no 'one size fits all' but the proportions are about right – one day off for every six days worked. That's seven weeks every year, without including holidays. Time enough for rest and recreation. Time to go to the local football match. Time to see the latest film or go to the theatre. Time for a game of golf or a visit to the gym. Time to see the exhibition or visit the pub. Time to spend playing with the children or grand-children. Time for a romantic weekend with your partner. Time to read or listen to music. Time for a decent holiday with people we love. Time to flop in front of the TV and watch something stupid. Time to stay in bed late and read the papers. Time to recharge the batteries so that, when we go back to whatever we normally do for 'work', we are rested, refreshed and restored, instead of constantly running on empty.

Exercise

1 What do you actually do each day, each week and each year to rest, to be refreshed and to keep your body in good shape?

2 What do you most enjoy doing when you have time? How much time do you spend doing it?

3 Who are the special people with whom you enjoy different aspects of your leisure time? Why not talk to some of them about doing something, regularly, together?

Inability to work

Of course, not everyone looks forward to time away from the workplace. Many people who are unable to go out to work, for a variety of reasons, would love the opportunity. Redundancy, disability, mental-health issues, long-term illness, accident, early retirement, unemployment levels, to mention just a few. We live in a society where we tend to value others, and ourselves, according to the sort of paid work we do. We have not long met someone when we ask: 'What do you do?' Maybe we try and find out which university they went to and what degree they got? We perhaps wonder what position they hold, how much they are earning, and assess them accordingly. On the other hand, not having a job, or having one that is poorly paid or not highly rated by society, can often make us think that we are of little worth.

This scenario becomes even more marked as people grow older and are able to 'do' less and less. It is exacerbated by our mobility, as well as by medical science enabling us to live longer. The chances are that a frail, elderly person will have little or no family nearby and will increasingly see themselves, and be seen, as a 'burden'. I hear people say things like: 'Isn't she marvellous? She's 90 and still doing her own shopping!' – as if her ability still to do things defined her value. I heard recently of a middle-class woman in her 80s who turned up at a tattoo parlour. The tattoo artist was surprised to see her, as she was not representative of his normal clientele. Had she had a tattoo before? 'Never,' she said. Where would she like the tattoo? And what sort of tattoo would she like? 'I'd like,' she replied, 'in big letters, right across my chest, the words: "DO NOT RESUSCITATE!"' She did not want to end her days as an invalid or a 'burden'.

We have not deliberately chosen this state of affairs but we are in it whether we like it or not. I remember seeing a nurse wheeling a frail, elderly man in a nursing home. He had dinner down his shirt. His mouth hung open, his face a vacant stare. As she pushed him into his room I read the sign on the door: 'Professor Sir John Richardson' (not his real name but certainly his real title). None of us is immune to becoming unable to look after ourselves, nor from ending our days incontinent, confused, afraid or alone.

For the last two years of her life, my mum lived in a nursing home. One of the carers commented that many of the residents never had a single visitor; some despite having family nearby. James was such a man. As a result he had no will to live and decided, therefore, to starve himself to death. I was deeply moved one day at seeing one of the carers, a young woman from Sri Lanka, weeping as she knelt at his side, begging him to eat. 'Please, James, please,' she would say, 'eat some for me.' In the end he did begin to eat again 'for her', as he started to find some purpose in life again.

'Elderly' implies to us 'old and frail'. Yet in many other cultures 'Elder' is a term of respect, someone looked up to for wisdom and guidance. My Ugandan friend calls me 'Musee', which means 'old man'. In England 'old man' would be an insult for someone in their 50s. Yet in Uganda to be 'Musee' is to be honoured.

It is not just elderly people, either. Christmas at the Cathedral is a magnificent occasion, with thousands of people, wonderful music and spectacular services and events. Each year we have a Christingle service for Highfield, a special school for children with very severe learning disabilities. One girl, Louise, suffering from cerebral palsy and with a severe speech impediment, sang a solo. As she returned to her seat I overheard her talking to one of the teachers. 'I was terrified', she stammered, 'but I knew there were all those people behind me who had faith in me.' For me it was the highlight of Christmas. I came away inspired and blessed, even though, if I'm honest, I hadn't really wanted to go.

We seem to have managed to get our values upside down, valuing people for what they can do, rather than who they are in the sight of God. In so doing we have failed to grasp an amazing truth: it is not just that the broken, the lonely, the vulnerable, the frail need us, it is *we* who need *them*. 'For the healthy to be whole, we need to be touched by those who are sick.'[44] 'When you open yourself to the cry of the world it causes you suffering, especially when it breaks and empties you. But this is God's gift to us, and it makes us fully alive.'[45] This is not in any way to glorify suffering, which can be brutalizing and destructive. Yet suffering, as Viktor Frankl, Holocaust survivor, reminds us, is inevitable. It is how we deal with it, and how we deal with those who suffer, which reveals our true humanity. He quotes Dostoevsky who says: 'There is only one thing that I dread: not to be worthy of my sufferings.'[46]

Jean Vanier and the L'Arche communities bear witness to this, as do many who live and work among the marginalized, the poor, the vulnerable, the weak, the broken.[47] This should not surprise us, since God is most clearly revealed in a helpless baby, born in a cow-shed, and in a tortured, broken body, hanging on a cross to die. And what could be of more supreme worth than that?

Exercise

1 What makes you feel valued and affirmed?
2 Read the parable of the prodigal son (Luke 15.11–32). Which son do you most identify with – the irresponsible, idle, spendthrift younger son or the hardworking, responsible older son, resentful of his father's generosity to his 'waste' of a brother? Imagine the father coming out to you, whichever one you think you are, longing for you to come in and be with him. He does not come out to find you because of all your hard work, your achievements, your loyalty. And he comes out despite your many failures, which you keep on repeating, again and again. He comes out to find you simply because he loves you for your own sake. Dwell on that image and remind yourself of it again and again.

3 Think about some of the people around you – neighbours, friends, family, colleagues, church members. Do you value them for who they are or just for what they do? How might you affirm them in ways that are not related to what they do or do not achieve?

"strengthen us in goodness and help up to grow in wholeness as in Christ"

5

Transformation

———••—••———

> Abbot Lot came to Abbot Joseph and said: 'Father, according
> as I am able I keep my little rule, and my little fast, my prayer,
> my meditation and contemplative silence; and according as
> I am able I strive to cleanse my heart of evil thoughts: now, what
> more should I do?' The elder rose up in reply and stretched out
> his hands to heaven, and his fingers became like ten lamps of
> fire. He said: 'Why not be totally changed into fire?'[1]

The keeping of a rule is not an end in itself. It is not so that
we can feel more in control or that our lives might be in order.
It is not even so that we can feel closer to God. Its purpose is
transformation: that we may become more like Christ, set on
fire by God's Holy Spirit. Benedict calls this *conversatio morum*,
and it is one of the three Benedictine vows, along with Obedience
and Stability. It is not an easy concept to translate. It is not
about a one-off change. It is rather about an ongoing, life-
long openness to keep on being changed, with and by the
communities which we are committed to. The Rule of Taizé
exhorts us:

> Never stand still, go forward with your brethren, run towards
> the goal in the footsteps of Christ.[2] *— Rule of Taizé —*

At first sight this seems to be in conflict with Benedict's
call to stability and contentment. Yet, in fact, the two go hand
in hand, because this transformation is, at heart, forged in

the place where we live, the place to which we are called, in the humdrum and the ordinariness of life. It comes in learning to love the person who always manages to get under my skin. It comes in persevering through dark times. It comes in seeking to realize all the potential that God has put, not just in me, but in others. It comes in coping with the unpredictability and suffering life brings, in being open to the cost and painfulness of inner change and in discovering treasure in the most unexpected places and people. It comes in being overwhelmed by God's love and grace when we are at our lowest ebb and least expect it.

It is not something brought about by world travel, shopping, a career change, a new house or finding a partner – though all those things may contribute to it. This transformation is about an inner journey, a journey involving many deaths and many resurrections. It is not running away from, but facing up to, our inner life, the hidden self which often holds the pain and hurt that we would rather not explore. It is not a one-off event but a life-long process.

Commitment to being transformed is central to our flourishing. It is radically different from living for ourselves, from doing our own thing. Here the concept of 'repentance' is important. The Greek word for repentance, *metanoia*, literally means 'to turn around'. It is because we find it so difficult to keep on facing God (and in doing so facing the truth about ourselves) that we keep wandering off on our own path, 'doing our own thing'. This determination to keep turning God-wards, so that we might become more Christ-like, is the essence of the 'called life', the life of discipleship.

At a recent series of special 'schools days' at the Cathedral we asked children to write down their fears and hopes for the future. A surprising number were afraid of dying young, of climate change, of World War III. They expressed hopes about future careers, getting married, having kids, travelling, being well off, becoming famous. One girl said she hoped to have 'a house, a car, children and to be a hairdresser *and* a vet'. There is an advertising myth that says 'you can have it all' – career, partner, children, travel, freedom – but it is simply untrue. Some choices, if we take their consequences seriously, will mean that other choices are closed to us. If 'X' then not 'Y'. Yet even more important than the particular choices we make is how we live our lives. We might call this 'virtue'.

Virtue is about inner attitudes and responses, even to extreme conditions. 'Everything can be taken from a man but one thing: the last of the human freedoms – to choose one's attitude in any given set of circumstances, to choose one's way.'[3] This is poignantly revealed in the cult classic *Zen and the Art of Motorcycle Maintenance*, which is not so much about the outward journey across America on a motorbike, but about the search for quality of living within.[4] The second Anglican–Roman Catholic International Commission report, *Life in Christ*, reminds us that 'the fundamental moral question is not "what ought we to do" but "what kind of persons are we called to become".'[5]

As mentioned earlier, 'outstanding virtue' was seen as a characteristic of the monastic community founded by Etheldreda in Ely. I asked Janet, the person who translated this early account of the monastery from Latin, what it meant. 'Oh,' she said, 'it doesn't really mean what we think of as "virtue" today. It meant something like "the ability to perform miracles"!' This reminds me of when John the Baptist is in prison and sends his disciples to ask if Jesus is the Messiah. Jesus replies:

> Go and tell John what you hear and see: the blind see, the lame walk, lepers are cleansed, the deaf hear, the dead are raised and the poor have good news brought to them. And blessed is the one who takes no offence at me.[6]

In both these cases it would seem that virtue is self-evident, self-authenticating. It would also seem that, where virtue has a particularly profound quality, astounding things happen. The quality of life, and the closeness of that life to God, produces fruit that speaks for itself. Jesus tells people: 'A good tree cannot bear bad fruit nor a bad tree good fruit . . . You will know them by their fruits.'[7] St Paul outlines what that 'good fruit' is: 'The fruit of the Spirit is love, joy, peace, patience, kindness, generosity, faithfulness, gentleness and self control. Against such things there is no law.'[8] We have probably all met people in whose lives this 'outstanding virtue' is clearly seen: a depth of presence of God in someone, which leaves us humbled.

May worked all her life on the production-line at Cadbury's in Birmingham. She wasn't married and had no kids. She was never on the Church Council nor ever held any position worthy of note. Yet when she died over 500 people turned up for her funeral. She was a person who offered extraordinary hospitality to countless folk, young and old. The door of her small terraced house was always open. She was 'Aunty May' to the whole community. In his funeral address the vicar referred to her as a 'mighty prayer warrior', and so she was. She was a mighty 'care' warrior as well. A life defined not by achievement but by virtue. Not by status but by hundreds of lives, deeply touched by her kind, smiling, generous, godly, prayerful, unassuming life.

Whether we live on a council estate or in a leafy suburb; whether we work as a cleaner or a consultant surgeon; whether we find a partner and have kids, live on our own or in community; whether we move across the world or stay in the village where we were born, important as these things are, they are nothing like so important as the quality of the lives we lead. And quality is not about achievement. It does not need to parade itself on a CV or defend itself if challenged. It is about virtue, an inner quality which does not need to be displayed or 'strutted', but which is self-evident, something we clearly recognize when we see it.

When I arrive at the pearly gates I do not think that God will be too bothered about my job title, qualifications, final salary or CV, but, rather, what sort of life I lived. There will be no need – nor point – in defending ourselves. In fact, defensiveness seems to be something remarkably lacking in Jesus. To Pilate, the High Priest and Herod's frustration, as the prophet Isaiah foretold:

> He opened not his mouth.
> Like a lamb led to slaughter
> Like a sheep that before its shearers is silent
> He did not open his mouth.[9]

Unfortunately defensiveness is a quality all too present in me, necessary to offset the lack of self-evident 'virtue'. What is important is not what we do, but how we live. Not the list of achievements on the CV but the quality of the life. Not what I say about myself but what is clearly evident to everyone else. Not status, but virtue.

And what is clearly evident to everyone else is of huge importance. Because, whether we like it or not, how we live will be a model for people to follow. Parents and grandparents, uncles and aunts, brothers and sisters, friends, teachers, our GP, the local vicar, neighbours. We are far more likely to follow their example, for better or for worse, than to do what they say.

We need to ask ourselves the question: 'What sort of rule will sustain and transform my life, my family, my workplace, my church, my community?' But perhaps an even more important question is: 'What sort of life am I modelling for my children, my family, my friends, my peers, colleagues and those who look to me for an example?' Am I happy to say: 'follow me'? Or would it be better if they didn't? I suspect the answer for most of us is a bit of each. As a former colleague of mine used to say: 'Learn from me. Learn from me as an example. And if you can't learn from me as an example, learn from me as a warning.' The problem is, we could do with a lot more examples and fewer warnings.

Exercise

1 Think of a couple of people who you have really looked up to, who have really influenced your life. What is it about them that makes them special?

2 If you could change one thing about yourself in order to be more Christ-like, what would it be? Why not talk to someone you trust, perhaps your 'Soul Friend', about how you might set about making such a change.

A big vision

Every year, in my previous job, we held an Advent Assembly at the local infants school. It proved to be the most popular assembly of the year, for both parents and children. Everyone sat around a series of low tables in the centre of the school hall. On the tables were around a hundred candles, of all shapes and sizes, flickering in the darkness. The atmosphere was magic. Each class presented their own special candle, representing their prayers for a sick classmate, for people who were homeless, for someone's grandma in hospital, for people in wars, or whatever their class had been especially concerned about. Every year we sang the same songs, including 'Jesus bids us shine with a pure, clear light', which I really quite liked, apart from the last line, which runs: 'You in your small corner, and I in mine.' Virtue does not imply that we don't need to use our gifts to the full or that we can simply sit back quietly 'in our small corner' and not worry about the big picture.

My friend Grace was a nun. I hadn't realized that nuns had holidays, but apparently they do. Each year Grace went on holiday with a friend she'd known for years. Her friend thought nuns led far too sheltered a life, so she always arranged adventure holidays to shake the cobwebs off Grace, for a couple of weeks at least. One such holiday involved white-water canoeing in the Canadian Rockies. Unfortunately the rapids proved even more challenging than they had thought. Halfway down, careering out of control, the canoe crashed fiercely into a rock. Grace was thrown to one side, causing the gold ring, the sign of her monastic vows, to fly off her finger and disappear into the foam. 'Oh, my ring, my ring,' she cried in despair. Her friend, above the thunder of the waters, yelled back: 'Stuff the ring. We're drowning!'

Actually, a lot of people are drowning. They are drowning of poverty and war, of abuse and violence, of injustice and discrimination, of neglect and lack of love. And the earth is drowning, literally, as we consume its resources at an unsustainable rate and face global warming and flooding of our own making. And there we are, in our small corner, worrying about a tiny ring, or some other such thing.

The quality of our lives needs to encompass and respond to the big picture. We need to seek inner virtue, but also have a big, outward-looking vision, too. That is not to say that each of us needs to tackle every problem, which is, of course, impossible. But each of us can respond with generosity and urgency to the pressing needs that surround us, playing our part in the 'big picture'. When Bob Geldof met Mother Teresa he was both impressed and daunted by her work. 'I could never do what you do,' he said. She held his hand and said: 'Remember this. I can do something you can't do and you can do something I can't do. But we both have to do it.'[10]

However, it is very easy for us to be consumed with our own small world and to be fearful of anything that might threaten it. Yet fear is a poor motive for doing – or not doing – anything. In many ways fear is the very opposite of faith, which might best be defined as 'courageous faithfulness'. When the angels appear to Mary, Joseph and the shepherds in the Gospel nativity narratives, the message is always the same: 'Do not be afraid.' Do not be afraid of the big change which is coming. Do not be afraid of responding to God's call. But a positive response requires courageous faithfulness, stepping out, beyond our comfort zone, into unknown territory. Stepping out beyond our fear of difference or loss of identity. Stepping out beyond our fear of failure or the fear of getting involved. Stepping out beyond our own 'small corner' into God's big vision for his creation. As President Roosevelt famously said: 'The only thing we have to fear is fear itself.'[11] After all, 'He is no fool who gives what he cannot keep to gain what he cannot lose.'[12]

John O'Donohue says that one of the greatest sins is the unlived life. He suggests that we spend such a long time worrying about not 'falling into sin' that we fail to live imaginatively, creatively, positively. We fail to dream dreams and pursue them. He quotes the second-century theologian, Irenaeus, who says: 'The glory of God is the human person fully alive.'[13] John O'Donohue sadly died in 2007, but he certainly lived a life of quality and creativity, and he inspired many others to live it too.

Our huge interest in celebrity, however, suggests that many of us are not 'fully alive'. Instead we seem to live vicariously through the people we read about or watch on TV. To live fully and authentically ourselves, even if we never get on *Big Brother* and are never mentioned in *Hello!* magazine, is surely better than trying to live out our fantasies through others. God calls each of us to live out the dream he is longing for us to find.

'I have come so that you can have life', says Jesus, 'and live it to the full.'[14]

People say 'life's too short'. They often mean that we should enjoy ourselves as much as possible while we can. The death of our son Tom, in 2002, made us feel acutely that life is too short to waste. We need to live it well, live it to the full, make it count, live it for others. Helder Camara, the former Roman Catholic Archbishop of Recife in Brazil, exhorts us: 'Live for that which we will never see.' Viktor Frankl says: 'It did not really matter what we expected from life, but rather, what life expected from us.'[15]

Exercise

1 What is your 'big vision'? What are your greatest hopes and dreams? What do you long for, for yourself, your loved ones, your church, your community, the world? Why not discuss this question with people you are close to, and with your church community?

2 To what extent is your life focused on the 'big picture' rather than the 'small corner'? Do you need to change this balance? If so, how might you go about doing it?

Interruptions

My ordination retreat in 1989 involved an interview with the Bishop. I was not looking forward to it. The trouble was, the Bishop was an erudite man who spoke a language I simply could not understand. Six months previously I had attended a lecture by him on the poetry of Geoffrey Hill. My only comfort was that, after half an hour, feeling utterly lost, I glanced at the A4 pad of my colleague Tim, who was taking notes. He had written, in large letters, across the page, 'I'm too stupid even to know when to laugh at the jokes!'

And now, here I am in the Bishop's study. He is going on about an academic article on 'Contemporary Cynicism' and I am desperately trying to concentrate because, in a minute, he will ask me what my view is on the subject. Luckily, I survive the interview almost unscathed. I've only got to survive lunch at the Bishop's house the following day, without spilling red wine on his carpet, and I should be OK. But when we arrive for lunch the Bishop isn't there. His wife welcomes us in, provides a lovely meal and informs us that the Bishop has cancelled all his engagements in order to spend the day at the bedside of someone who is dying. I felt so privileged to have experienced that very different side of him. But it was not the only thing I was grateful for. It was an important reminder that what is in the diary is not always that which is most important.

Our regular routine of prayer and faithful service, the agenda full of worthy commitments, is fine. Until something interrupts us. A phone call. The knock on the door. A cyclist is hit by a car just as you are on the way to an important meeting. The lady next door falls and breaks her hip. You arrive at work with a punishing day in prospect and find your secretary in floods of tears because her husband has just left her.

These things are not always so obvious – as with David and the man who had come to ask him to bury his daughter (p. 37). Such 'interruptions' are not separate from our lives. They are not unfortunate distractions that prevent us doing the real business. The Conservative Prime Minister, Harold Macmillan, was once asked what was most likely to blow governments off course. He replied: 'Events!' How we tackle those 'events' – Princess Diana's death, 9/11, or the countless unforeseen happenings which interrupt our schedule, our priorities – reveals a lot about who we are. Things happen, or, as some people unknowingly describe the doctrine of the Fall, 'shit happens'. It happens on a national and international scale. It happens at the local level. It happens to us, personally. And it is how we deal with the unexpected, the inconvenient, the disruptive, which tends to reveal the 'quality' or 'virtue' of our lives.

This seems to be at the heart of the Northumbria Community,[16] whose rule is a consideration of two words – 'Availability' and 'Vulnerability'. It depends on what Jean-Pierre de Caussade[17] called the 'Sacrament of the Present Moment', an attitude of attentiveness which makes us utterly present to this moment, in this place, with this person, rather than looking over their shoulder to see if anyone more interesting or important is about to enter the room. 'Be present to the time in which you live. Adapt yourself to the conditions of the moment.'[18] Such availability is costly. It interrupts the flow of our lives. It messes up our schedule. It eats away at our time and upsets our rhythm. A friend told me: 'I am ferocious with my use of time!' The reality for many of us is this: we live at such a pace that, when something 'interrupts' us, there is no slack in the system to deal with it, and we may well be overwhelmed.

Jesus' life is full of interruptions. People stop him on the road. They break into the house where he is speaking. They stop him going off to get some peace and quiet. His family turn up and demand some of his attention. A woman caught in adultery (where is the man, we may ask?) is dragged in front of him. The Pharisees try and trap him when he is off guard. People bring children to him when it's not convenient. It's getting late and the crowd has no food. A woman pours costly perfume all over him while he is trying to eat his dinner. I bet it put him right off the fish. In fact, his ministry is constantly interrupted. He is not, however, ultimately diverted by interruptions from the clear, strategic path he knows he must walk. They interrupt him and he responds to those interruptions, but they do not knock him off course.

Such incidents are the very stuff of life, which turns out not to be anything like as orderly as we'd no right to expect it would be anyway. And the interruptions are not always small or trivial. There is an unwritten Western myth that goes something like this: You are born into a loving family, have a great childhood and education, embark on a successful career, meet the right partner who sticks with you for the rest of your life, buy a lovely home, have 2.4 children who grow up happy and well, you avoid serious illness or any other disaster and, finally, you die in your sleep, fulfilled and content, aged 93. Frankly, I don't know anyone like that at all!

Most of us will experience untimely death, serious illness, financial strife, a serious accident, breakdown of relationship or some other terrible difficulty or tragedy. Yet when they occur we often ask 'why is this happening to me?' If we lived in Zimbabwe, Afghanistan, the Balkans or the Gaza Strip, we would know that these things are not abnormal or anomalous. Suffering is part of what it means to be human in a fallen world. And it is not that people in those places find such events less painful. It is that they expect them and know they must live with pain as well as joy, loss as well as gain. They have probably learned these things in a community where suffering is ever present, where there is a sense of solidarity in suffering. By contrast, in the West, when suffering comes we ask 'why me?' It often only serves to increase our sense of isolation.

The book of Job is the Bible's major treatise on suffering. We see the devastating 'interruption' of Job's upright, but thus far uneventful, life as first his family and property are struck down and then his own health is destroyed. Job cries out for God to answer the question 'why?' However, he never receives an answer to that question. Job is a complex book, dealing with a difficult and complex theme that we can only touch upon here. However, two things do emerge from Job's sufferings. First, Job realizes that serving God is not about reward: it must be for its own sake, no matter what the consequence. 'Shall we receive the good at the hand of the Lord and not the bad also?' Job replies to his embittered wife.[19] This is an important question. Are we prepared to serve God for nothing? Like Shadrach, Meshach and Abednego, who say to King Nebuchadnezzar: 'Our God whom we serve is able to deliver us ... but if not, we will still not worship your Gods.'[20] The Rule of Taizé says: 'He who lives in mercy ... gives himself simply, in self forgetfulness, joyfully, with all his heart, freely, expecting nothing in return.'[21]

Second, it is through disaster, pain and misfortune that Job meets with God more profoundly than he has ever done before. 'I had heard of you by the hearing of the ear', he says, 'but now my eyes have seen you.'[22] There is no guarantee of this. Suffering is sometimes so great that it seems to be utterly brutalizing and destructive. It can take many generations to recover from. Yet it is often through those painful, terrible interruptions, where our faith is most severely tested, that we meet with God, in the depths, in what St John of the Cross and other spiritual writers call 'the dark night of the soul'.[23]

How we get on when these 'interruptions' suddenly confront us will depend on how we have lived beforehand. In Philip Marsden's travels across Russia, in search of the 'Old Believers', he relates a conversation between the priest and a struggling disciple. 'It's not the rules that are important, Sasha,' said Father Gyorgi, 'but the obeying of them. These rules are a way of practising discipline. If you can keep up with the small rules then, when the bigger questions come, it will be easier to make the right choice.'[24] 'Do not fear to share the trials of others nor be afraid of suffering', says Brother Roger, 'for it is often at the bottom of the abyss that perfection of joy is given in communion with Jesus Christ.'[25]

It is not so much how we respond to these 'interruptions' that reveals the quality of our lives. It is rather that the quality of our lives determines how we deal with the interruptions when they come, which they inevitably will.

Exercise

Think of a couple of occasions when your schedule was seriously interrupted by something unexpected which you simply had to respond to – one you felt you dealt with well and one badly. What do these incidents tell you about yourself?

6

Beginning

———•◆•———

A brother who had withdrawn and taken the habit shut himself up saying 'I am an anchorite'... (but) the old men made him go round all the brethren's cells, bowing before them and saying: 'Forgive me, for I am not an anchorite. I am a beginner.'[1]

It may seem strange to have a chapter entitled 'Beginning' at the end of a book. Most of us still have a very long way indeed to travel on our journey. Yet the realization of this at least suggests progress. Like the eager young man who, after proudly announcing that he has become a monk, quickly realizes that he is, in fact, only a beginner. For the Desert Fathers, and many other serious disciples before and since, the more they advance, the more they become aware of their own failings and realize just how far they have still to go. It is as we draw closer to Christ that his light reveals the darkness in us. Like Peter, who, after seeing the miraculous catch of fish, says to Jesus: 'Away from me, Lord, for I am a sinful man.'[2]

Benedict is quite clear about the fact that his Rule is not so much for the mature but for beginners. It is in his final chapter that he says:

Whoever you are, then, who are hurrying forward to your heavenly Father, with Christ's help fulfil this little rule, which is written for beginners.[3]

It is only after we have lived our rule well that: 'You will come at the end . . . to those heights of learning and virtue we have mentioned above.'[4] Don Paterson, in his book about sonnets, says: 'The poets had to learn the rules before they could deliberately break them.'[5]

To become faithful, wise disciples who are on easy terms with our creator, and with his creatures, requires of us a lifetime of discipline and perseverance. When I was at school a boy called Clegg played the oboe in the school orchestra. I was captivated by the rich, deep sound and thought 'one day I will learn to play the oboe'. I was reminded of this some years later, being moved to tears by the film *The Mission*, portraying the desperate plight of the indigenous people, sacrificial pawns in the hands of superpower politics, reflected in the haunting music of Gabriel's oboe. Yet, 45 years later, despite feeling that same longing to play the oboe on many occasions since, I have yet to pick up the oboe or practise a single note.

I want to be able to play, but I don't want to practise. To play an instrument well, so that others can enjoy your playing, so that you can improvise and break the rules and just allow yourself to be lost in the music, does not happen overnight. It takes years of practice. Day after day. We live next door to the boys who sing in the Cathedral choir. Each morning they are up at the crack of dawn, practising instruments before going off to breakfast, then choir rehearsal, then school, then back for tea, then another rehearsal, then evensong, then supper, then homework and bed. It is a life of discipline and community, which they seem, for the most part, thoroughly to enjoy. And it yields the great fruit of a lifetime of enjoyment in creating music. One of these days, perhaps, I will pick up that oboe.

Discipleship is such a venture. It will need daily discipline and ongoing perseverance. It will not come easily to most of us. Like Job, we will often feel God is silent and impossible to reach. Sometimes, the great certainties we believed in will be rocked to the core, and, in the darkness, we will need to let them go in order to find a deeper truth. We will often fail and fall short. Yet what is offered to us is nothing less than everything. Not just some vague hope of future happiness but the promise of life, authentic life. Life lived now, but with eternal consequences. Life lived for ourselves. And life lived for others. Life lived with Christ, in all its fullness.

Jesus has been speaking in parables. They are enigmatic and difficult to understand. He asks his disciples: 'Have you understood all this?' 'Yes,' they reply (probably not wanting to admit the truth that they have no idea what he is on about). 'Well then,' says Jesus, 'every teacher of the law who becomes a learner in the Kingdom of heaven is like a householder who can produce from his store things old and new.'[6]

Even those of us who are teachers must start again and become learners in the Kingdom of Heaven, so that we can keep on discovering all of the riches Christ offers us, things new, things recently discovered and experienced. And things old, ancient wisdom from the Bible, from the desert, from Benedict and from many other sources.

At the end of his long spiritual pilgrimage, T. S. Eliot, in *The Four Quartets*, finds himself once more, albeit with new insights, back at the beginning.[7] When it comes to serious discipleship, most of us have hardly started. Like the novice in the desert we find ourselves saying:

Forgive me. I am not an anchorite. I am a beginner.

Exercise

1 Go back to the form in the Introduction (p. xvii). You may wish to fill it in again. Why not fill it in together with some close friends or a group from church?

2 Mark in red the things you plan to stop doing right now.
3 Mark in orange the things you need to think about and, perhaps, change.
4 Write in green the new things you will now definitely commit yourself to doing.
5 Rewrite your summary of your own 'Rule of Life', preferably with others. Think about how you might try and live it out, together. You may find that you want to work on different 'Rules' for some of the different groups you belong to: close family, cell group, church, workplace, etc.

Postscript

Margaret is a single woman, retired now. She spent most of her life as a missionary. She relates to us a story about her childhood, when she was ten years old. One day, on her way home from school, she looks in the local jewellers' shop and sees a silver locket. 'What a wonderful present that would be for my mum,' she thinks. But it costs £1/10 shillings (£1.50p) and she only gets a shilling a week pocket money (5p in today's money). But she decides she will save up and buy it for her mum's next birthday. It means saving most of her pocket money each week for nearly a year. It means doing without a lot of things she would have really liked to buy. She puts aside the money each week in a little box in her bedroom. At first it hardly seems like anything at all, as if she'll never get there. But she keeps on putting it in, week after week. Almost a year later, as her mum's birthday approaches, she reaches her target. She walks to the jewellers, asks for the locket and pours out the pile of coins on the counter. The jeweller counts out the money and hands her the locket. She goes home and carefully wraps up the tiny parcel. On her mum's birthday Margaret comes down to breakfast and hands her mum the tiny, neatly wrapped parcel. She waits, heart thumping, red-faced, wondering how her mum will react. Her mum carefully removes the paper and opens the tiny box. She stares in disbelief at this precious, costly gift. She looks at Margaret and back at the box. She bursts into tears, her heart full of gratitude, pride and love. And so does Margaret. And so does her dad. They are caught up together, in each other's arms, in a moment which will deepen their relationships and strengthen their love for one another in a most profound way. Something they will remember all of their lives. Something which will help sustain them through all the years of separation, with Margaret working overseas. And, of course, the paradox is that what Margaret has given her mum did, in fact, come from her mum anyway, because it was her mum who gave her the pocket money, week after week, in the first place.

Following a rule can be difficult. It needs discipline, perseverance. Yet what we are offering to God is not our own. It is simply what we ourselves have received at God's hands through his amazing, generous grace. By offering it back, through the discipline of our lives, expressed in the rule we live by, there are no losers. Love and grace are not diminished by being offered up and given away. Rather they grow and blossom and flourish. And the world is a better place. And everyone is blessed.

Appendix 1

The Community of St Etheldreda, Ely Cathedral

A simple rule for living

Etheldreda came to Ely in AD 673 and founded a religious community of men and women. The quality of her life and miracles attributed to her, even after her death, attracted pilgrims from far and wide, to what was then a remote and inaccessible place.

The Saxon monastery was destroyed by the Danes in 870 but rebuilt by Benedictines in 970. Around 1080 work began on what is now Ely Cathedral.

The monks lived their common life according to the Rule written by St Benedict in the sixth century.

For us in the twenty-first century, living hectic lives with many demands in a complex world, the task of finding a simple rule to live by, to keep us rooted in Christ and living for him, is all the more essential. The principles behind Benedict's Rule are just as relevant today as they were 1500 years ago.

Benedict's Rule has at its heart a careful balance of the following major disciplines:

Listening: the call to listen to God through his word, through silence, through quiet days and retreats, through others, through prayer and through corporate worship, which is the real 'Work of God'.

Obedience: the Latin root means 'to listen intently' to God. Those who hear the word are called to let it shape their lives.

Stability: important for us in an age of constant change – the need to belong and to be content within a stable Christian community, learning to live together in love even with those we find most difficult.

Work: the call to reflect God's creative activity, including practical service, however humble, for the benefit of all.

Transformation: a commitment to be changed, to see the need for it, to seek to realize all the potential that God has put within us, to be open to God's transforming love and grace in us, to become more Christ-like.

Act of Commitment:
Lord Jesus Christ, trusting in your love and grace, and wanting to find a pattern of living to guide me in your way,

I . . . .

commit myself to:

- **listen:** to God through daily prayer, reading God's word, silence and regular times of retreat.
- **obedience:** to listen intently to God, particularly with the help of a spiritual director or soul friend who can accompany me on my journey.
- **stability:** by being part of an ongoing community where I can meet Christ in others and be challenged by those who know me well.
- **work:** in my daily life seeking to serve others in practical ways and proclaiming his kingdom of justice and peace.
- **transformation:** by being prepared to change, to see the need for it in myself, to be constantly open to the transforming fire of God's love.

Appendix 2

Ely Cursillo Rule of Life

Living in the Love and Grace of Christ

Lord Jesus Christ, knowing that you love me and have redeemed me,

I . . . .

from this day forward, a living and growing member of your mystical body, in union with all Christians, with the help of your grace, will contribute my idealism, my self-surrender, my service and my love to hasten the coming of your Kingdom in me and in the World.

I acknowledge that this Rule is an act of solemn dedication which I make in the name of the Father and of the Son and of the Holy Spirit, Amen.

My Rule of Life

Jesus prayed: 'I pray for all those who believe in me, that they may all be one, Father . . . so the world may believe that you have sent me . . . and that you love them just as you love me' (*from John 17*).

Prayer, worship and study
What will I do every day, every week, every month, every year to deepen my spiritual journey?

Action
What will I do, by my words, my attitudes and in practical ways, to reach out with God's love and grace to my friends and family, to my colleagues, to my community, to the wider world?

Health and well-being
What will I do to keep myself healthy and to promote healthy relationships with those closest to me?

Suggested Order for Reunions

All: **Come Holy Spirit, fill the hearts of your faithful and kindle in us the fire of your love.**

Leader: Send forth your Spirit and we shall be created.

All: **And you shall renew the face of the earth.**

Leader: Let us pray.

All: **O God, who by the light of the Holy Spirit did instruct the hearts of the faithful, grant that by the same Holy Spirit we may be truly wise and ever enjoy His consolations, through Jesus Christ our Lord. Amen.**

The Lord's Prayer may be said.

Prayer and study
'You shall love the Lord your God with all your heart.'
What have you done this week which has helped your spiritual journey?
When did you feel closest to Christ?
What have you found most difficult?

Action
'You shall love your neighbour as yourself.'
What have you done this week to reach out with God's love

to friends and family . . . . ?
to colleagues . . . . ?
to your community . . . . ?
to the wider world . . . . ?
Were there any encouragements?
Is there an issue you are really struggling with?
What hopes do you have for the coming week?

Health and well-being
What have you done to keep yourself and your close relationships healthy?

Prayer:
for one another
for members of the group not able to be present
for those on our hearts
for wider issues in our communities and our world.

Prayer of Thanksgiving:
We give you thanks, Almighty God, for all the benefits you have given us. You will live and reign for ever and ever. Amen.

Appendix 3

---·•◆•·---

Summary of the Rule of the Northumbria Community

This is the Rule we embrace. This is the Rule we will keep: we say YES to AVAILABILITY; we say YES to VULNERABILITY.

We are called to be **AVAILABLE** to God and to others:

Firstly to be available to God in the **cell** of our own heart when we can be turned towards Him, and seek His face;
then to be available to others in a call to exercise **hospitality**, recognizing that in welcoming others we honour and welcome the Christ Himself;
then to be available to others through participation in His care and concern for them, by praying and **interceding** for their situations in the power of the Holy Spirit;
then to be available for participation in **mission** of various kinds according to the calling and initiatives of the Spirit.

We are called to intentional, deliberate **VULNERABILITY**:

We embrace the vulnerability of being **teachable** expressed in:

a discipline of prayer;
exposure to Scripture;
a willingness to be accountable to others in ordering our ways and our heart in order to effect change.

We embrace the responsibility of taking the **heretical imperative:**

by speaking out when necessary or asking awkward questions that will often upset the status quo;
by making relationships the priority, and not reputation.

We embrace the challenge to live as **church without walls**, living openly amongst unbelievers and other believers in a way that the life of God in ours can be seen, challenged or questioned. This will involve us building friendships outside our Christian ghettos or club-mentality, not with ulterior evangelistic motives, but because we genuinely care.

Appendix 4

_____·•◆•·_____

The Rule of the Iona Community

Our five-fold Rule calls us to:

1 Daily Prayer and Bible reading
2 Sharing and accounting for the use of our money
3 Planning and accounting for the use of our time
4 Action for Justice and Peace in society
5 Meeting with and accounting to each other.

1. Daily Prayer and Bible Reading

We are asked to pray for each other, for our common concerns, and for the wider work of the Church, on a daily basis. We are also asked to read the Bible on a regular and frequent basis. Together with prayer requests and topics in the Members' booklet, the use is commended of _Pray Now_ (published by St Andrew Press) or _With All God's People_ (published by the WCC, Geneva).

2. Sharing and Accounting for the Use of Our Money

(a) We are asked, first, to account to each other for the use of our income.
(b) We are then asked, in Family Groups, to agree our individual baseline commitments and special circumstances and expenses: thus arriving at a personal disposable income figure from which the amount to be given (a tithe – 10% in most cases) can be deducted.
(c) The amount to be given should be divided up as follows:
   (i) to the wider work of the Church, and to bodies concerned with promoting justice and peace, world development, etc. – 60%
   (ii) to the work of the Iona Community – 20%
   (iii) to purposes decided by the Family Group – 10%

(iv) to purposes decided by the Common Fund Trustees on behalf
of the Community – 5%
(v) to the Travel Pool – 5%.

The accounting year for each of these amounts is from 1st January
to 31st December.

3. Planning and Accounting for the Use of Our Time
This discipline seems to have its origins in the early days of the
Community, when craftsmen doubted the ability of ministers to
work an eight-hour 'shift'! Through it, we are all asked to plan our
time, in such a way that proper 'weighting' is given, not simply to
work, but equally to leisure, to time for family, to developing
skills or acquiring new ones, to worship and devotion, to voluntary
work – and to sleep!

4. Action for Justice and Peace in Society
Our act of commitment on justice and peace is, as was also said of
the earlier Act of Commitment on Peace, 'a point of departure'. It will
remain no more than a pious hope (and a false witness) unless we
seek, separately and together, to put it into practice.

Justice and Peace Commitment
We believe:

1 that the Gospel commands us to seek peace founded on justice
and that costly reconciliation is at the heart of the Gospel;
2 that work for justice, peace and an equitable society is a matter of
extreme urgency;
3 that God has given us partnership as stewards of creation and that
we have a responsibility to live in a right relationship with the
whole of God's creation;
4 that, handled with integrity, creation can provide for the needs of
all, but not for the greed which leads to injustice and inequality,
and endangers life on earth;
5 that everyone should have the quality and dignity of a full life that
requires adequate physical, social and political opportunity, without
the oppression of poverty, injustice and fear;

6 that social and political action leading to justice for all people and encouraged by prayer and discussion, is a vital work of the Church at all levels;

7 that the use or threatened use of nuclear and other weapons of mass destruction is theologically and morally indefensible and that opposition to their existence is an imperative of the Christian faith.

As Members and Family Groups we will:

1 engage in forms of political witness and action, prayerfully and thoughtfully, to promote just and peaceful social, political and economic structures;

2 work for a British policy of renunciation of all weapons of mass destruction and for the encouragement of other nations, individually or collectively, to do the same;

3 celebrate human diversity and actively work to combat discrimination on grounds of age, colour, disability, mental well-being, differing ability, gender, colour, race, ethnic and cultural background, sexual orientation or religion;

4 work for the establishment of the United Nations Organization as the principal organ of international reconciliation and security, in place of military alliances;

5 support and promote research and education into non-violent ways of achieving justice, peace and a sustainable global society;

6 work for reconciliation within and among nations by international sharing and exchange of experience and people, with particular concern for politically and economically oppressed nations.

5. Meeting with and Accounting to Each Other
We are asked to do this

(a) In Family Groups
(b) In Plenaries.

We are also asked to give a written undertaking each year (through the 'With-us' card) that we are 'with the Community' in commitment to the Rule.

Appendix 5

Moot Rhythm of Life (see www.moot.uk.net)

We live the moot rhythm of life through presence, acceptance, creativity, balance, accountability and hospitality.

Presence

We commit to journeying together with God and each other, by meeting together as a community, in prayer in worship, friendship, grief, and happiness. Being a hopeful sign of an open community in the city rather than just a group of individuals or anonymous people.

Acceptance

We desire to accept both ourselves and other people as they are, and to allow people to say what they believe without fear of judgement. We want to create a safe space where people feel at home and welcomed. We hope to learn from all those in and outside the community.

Creativity

We want to have an open approach to how we learn, live and encounter God in the plurality of our city and the world. We wish to be creative in our worship, in prayer, in our lives, in learning, and with the Christian tradition, in our theology and with the arts.

Balance

We aspire to live with integrity in the city, striving as a community for balance between work, rest and play. We wish to develop healthy spiritual disciplines such as daily prayer, meditation and contemplation, drawing on the ancient Christian paths. We want to live within our means, living sustainable lives. We desire to not be simply consumers, but people committed to giving and receiving in all of life.

Accountability
Within the rhythm of life we desire to be accountable to one another, to grow and journey together, listening to each other and the wider Christian community for wisdom rather than trusting only ourselves. We want to have a willingness to share life, rather than to privatize it and we seek to walk together in a deep way rather than as strangers who only know the surface of each other.

Hospitality
We wish to welcome all whom we encounter, when we are gathered and when we are dispersed, extending Christ's gracious invitation to relationship, meaning and life in all its fullness.

Practices
As we seek to live out this rhythm in our own lives we commit to joining the community for prayer each day at 12 noon, and being part of a small prayer group.

Notes

————•◆•————

1 Dietrich Bonhoeffer, letter to his brother, Karl-Friedrich, 1935.

Preface

1 E.g. *Seeking God*, Esther de Waal, Fount, 1984. For a more devotional approach see *Seven Sacred Pauses*, Macrina Wiederkehr, Sorin Books, 2008.

2 *Ecclesiogenesis*, Leonardo Boff, Orbis, 1986, p. 63.

Introduction

1 Acts 2.44; 4.32.

2 Acts 2.45, 47; 4.33, 34.

3 See *Living Together in A World Falling Apart*, Dave and Neta Jackson, Creation House, 1974 and *Celebration of Discipline*, Richard Foster, Hodder and Stoughton, 1978 – an important book that introduced a generation of evangelicals to ancient spiritual wisdom.

1 A personal journey

1 *Common Prayer Collection*, Michael Leunig, Collins Dove, 1993.

2 Psalm 19.8–10.

3 Matthew 7.3.

4 John 17.20ff.: Jesus prays for the disciples: 'May they all be one, just as you, Father, are in me and I in you, may they also be in us.'

5 See Appendix 4.

6 *The Wisdom of the Desert* and *The Sayings of the Desert Fathers* have been translated by Thomas Merton (Shambhala, 1960) and Benedicta Ward (SLG, 1975). See also the excellent book by Rowan

Williams, *Silence and Honey Cakes*, Lion, 2003. Also William Dalrymple's *From the Holy Mountain*, Flamingo, 1998, a fascinating insight into the earliest Christian monastic communities and their modern-day successors.

7 See www.cursillo.org.uk and www.ukcursillo.org.

8 See Appendix 2.

9 For a fuller discussion of this issue see *A Churchless Faith*, Alan Jamieson, SPCK, 2002. See also www.spiritedexchanges.org.uk, a network for those who have left or are on the fringes of church.

10 Theology of Evangelism Conference, St John's College, Durham, March 2001.

11 See www.moot.uk.net.

12 See www.northumbriacommunity.org.

13 See Appendix 1.

14 *Liber Eliensis*, trans. Janet Fairweather, Boydell, 2005.

15 See the Northumbria Community Rule for a discussion of what they call the 'Heretical Imperative . . . speaking out when necessary or asking awkward questions that will often upset the status quo . . . making relationships the priority, and not reputation' (www.northumbriacommunity.org).

16 I am grateful to Peter Sills for a series of lectures at Ely Cathedral which introduced me to Benedict and his Rule.

17 For example, the 'Stylites', followers of St Simeon Stylites who lived on top of pillars to avoid all direct contact with others in their attempts to draw close to God.

2 Listen

1 Rule of Benedict, Prologue.

2 Rule of Benedict, Chapter VI.

3 Rule of Taizé, Prayer, Taizé, 1968.

4 See *From the Holy Mountain*, William Dalrymple, Flamingo, 1998.

5 Genesis 28.17.

6 Hebrews 12.1–2.

7 *The Word of God?*, Keith Ward, SPCK, 2010.

8 'Season of Blood', in *Letter to Daniel*, Fergal Keane, Penguin, 1996.

9 Collect for Second Sunday in Advent, Book of Common Prayer.

10 See, e.g. *Sacred Reading, the Ancient Art of Lectio Divina*, Michael Casey, Liguori/Triumph, 1996.

11 Psalm 23, King James Version of the Bible.

12 *Message of the Psalms*, W. Brueggemann, Augsburg, 1984.

13 This is a phrase used by a friend of mine, a prison chaplain, about the painful lives of some of the inmates.

14 *If This Is a Man*, Primo Levi, Abacus, 1987.

15 Job 2.13.

16 *Anam Cara*, John O'Donohue, Bantam, 1997.

17 *A Thousand Reasons for Living*, Helder Camara, DLT, 1981.

18 See Mark 5.25–34.

19 Rule of Taizé, The Council, Taizé, 1968. See also *Doing Business with Benedict*, Dollard et al., Continuum, 2002.

20 *Eight Day Retreat with St Ignatius of Loyola*, Norbert Alcover, St Paul, 1989, p. 111.

21 *Sayings of the Desert Fathers*, trans. Thomas Merton, Shambhala, 1960.

22 See, for example: www.greenbelt.org.uk; www.walsingham.org.uk; www.walsinghamanglican.org.uk; www.springharvest.org; www. Taizé.fr; www.new-wine.org; www.iona.org.uk.

23 Rule of Taizé, The Spiritual Disciplines, Taizé, 1968.

24 *Silence and Honey Cakes*, Rowan Williams, Lion, 2003.

25 Rule of Taizé, The Spiritual Disciplines, Taizé, 1968.

26 Rule of Taizé, Preamble, Taizé, 1968.

27 Rule of Benedict, Chapter VI.

28 Rule of Taizé, The Spiritual Disciplines, Taizé, 1968.

29 James 1.19.

30 See, e.g. Rule of Benedict, Chapters IV, V, XXXIV and XL.

31 Mark 10.35–45.

32 Mark 14.3–9.

33 Rule of Benedict, Chapter LXVIII.
34 James 3.8–10.
35 1 Corinthians 6.12.
36 Ephesians 4.15, 25–27.
37 'Fleeing' in *Silence and Honey Cakes*, Williams.
38 *The Music of the Primes*, Marcus de Sautoy, Fourth Estate, 2003.
39 Rule of Benedict, Chapter XXXI.
40 Luke 6.41.
41 Luke 6.37–38.
42 *The Wisdom of the Desert*, Chapter XXXV, trans. Thomas Merton, Shambhala, 1960.
43 For a full and wonderful meditation on this parable see: *The Return of the Prodigal Son*, Henri Nouwen, Doubleday, 1992.
44 *Seeking God*, Esther de Waal, Fount, 1984.
45 Rule of Benedict, Prologue.
46 Luke 22.25–26.
47 John 13.1–11.
48 L'Oréal advert.
49 *The Cloister Walk*, Kathleen Norris, Lion, 1999.
50 See Romans 12.3.
51 Holy Communion Order One, *Common Worship*, Church House Publishing, 2000.
52 See Appendix 4.
53 Many retreat houses offer opportunities for Spiritual Direction. See also www.spidir.org.uk, which is an ecumenical network of people offering Spiritual Direction.
54 1 John 1.8.

3 Stability

1 Rule of Benedict, Chapter 1.
2 London *Metro*, 13 February 2008.
3 Rule of Taizé, The Prior, Taizé, 1968.
4 'The More Loving One', *Collected Poems*, W. H. Auden, Vintage, 1991. Used by permission of Faber and Faber.

5 2 Timothy 2.13.
6 Church of England marriage vows, *Common Worship: Pastoral Services*, Church House Publishing, 2000.
7 *Mere Christianity*, C. S. Lewis, Fount, 1952.
8 Philippians 2.12.

4 Work

1 Rule of Taizé, The Spiritual Disciplines, Taizé, 1968.
2 2 Thessalonians 3.10.
3 Luke 17.10.
4 *Common Worship*, Order One, Church House Publishing, 2000.
5 Matthew 10.39; Luke 6.20–21. See also *Finding Happiness*, Christopher Jamison, Weidenfeld and Nicolson, 2008.
6 John 3.26–30.
7 Rule of Taizé, Preamble, Taizé, 1968.
8 John 13.1–11.
9 *Seeking God*, Esther de Waal, Fount, 1984, Chapter 2.
10 Rule of Benedict, Chapter VII.
11 Rule of Benedict, Chapter VII.
12 Rule of Taizé, The Spiritual Disciplines, Taizé, 1968.
13 Matthew 6.3–4.
14 See for example Genesis 1.26–31; Mark 12.1–12; Luke 9.23; Luke 12.13–34; Galatians 5.22–23.
15 'Devotions', John Donne.
16 *Common Prayer Collection*, Michael Leunig, Collins Dove, 1993.
17 See Luke 9.1–6; 12.22–34.
18 Matthew 25.31–46.
19 See Rule of Benedict, Chapters IX, XXXIX, XL, LIII, LIV, LV.
20 See *An Inconvenient Truth*, a documentary film by Al Gore.
21 Luke 10.25–37.
22 *Affluenza*, Oliver James, Vermilion, 2007, Chapter 5.
23 See *Issues Facing Christians Today*, John Stott, Marshalls, 1984, Chapter 12.
24 Desmond Tutu, University sermon, Great St Mary's, Cambridge, 1993.

25 'Gratefulnesse', *The English Poems of George Herbert*, Everyman, 1974.
26 Rule of Taizé, Guests, Taizé, 1968.
27 Luke 14.12–14.
28 See www.acommonword.com.
29 See Hebrews 13.1–2.
30 Genesis 18.
31 'Song of a Man Who Has Come Through', *Complete Poems of D. H. Lawrence*, Wordsworth, 1994.
32 Leviticus 19.33–34.
33 See *The Common Good*, an excellent resource booklet with study guide, produced by the UK Catholic Bishops' Conference in 1996 prior to the General Election.
34 *Silence and Honey Cakes*, Rowan Williams, Lion, 2003, Chapter 2.
35 Matthew 25.31–46.
36 E.g. see Mark 1.35–39.
37 Mark 6.31–32.
38 Matthew 11.19.
39 John 2.1–11.
40 Mark 1.37–38.
41 Old Mars Bar slogan: 'A Mars a day helps you work, rest and play.'
42 Rule of Benedict, Chapter XLIX.
43 Genesis 2.2–3.
44 John Bell, Ely Cathedral, September 2007.
45 Mike Yaconelli, Greenbelt, August, 2007.
46 *Man's Search for Meaning*, Viktor Frankl, Rider, 1959.
47 See www.larche.org.uk and *The Broken Body*, Jean Vanier, DLT, 1988 and *Face to Face*, Frances Young, Epworth, 1985. Frances Young is a (retired) professor of theology whose son Arthur has severe learning and physical disabilities.

5 Transformations

1 *The Wisdom of the Desert*, trans. Thomas Merton, Shambhala, 1960.

2 Rule of Taizé, Preamble, Taizé, 1968.
3 *Man's Search for Meaning*, Viktor Frankl, Rider, 1959.
4 *Zen and the Art of Motorcycle Maintenance*, Robert Pirsig, Corgi, 1976.
5 *Life in Christ*, ARCIC II, 1994.
6 Matthew 11.2–6; see also John 10.37, 38.
7 Matthew 7.18–20.
8 Galatians 5.22.
9 Isaiah 53.7; Luke 23.8–9; John 19.8–9.
10 *God: What the Critics Say*, ed. Martin Wroe, Spire, 1992.
11 Inaugural Address, F. D. Roosevelt, 1933.
12 Attributed to Jim Elliot, missionary and martyr in Ecuador, 1927–56.
13 *Anam Cara*, John O'Donohue, Bantam, 1997.
14 Jesus' words in John 10.10.
15 *Man's Search for Meaning*, Frankl.
16 See www.northumbriacommunity.org.
17 *The Sacrament of the Present Moment*, J.-P. de Caussade, Harper, 1989.
18 Rule of Taizé, Preamble, Taizé, 1968.
19 Job 2.10.
20 Daniel 3.16–18.
21 Rule of Taizé, The Spiritual Disciplines, Taizé, 1968.
22 Job 42.5.
23 *Dark Night of the Soul*, St John of the Cross, Dover, 2003.
24 *The Spirit Wrestlers*, Philip Marsden, Flamingo, 1998.
25 Rule of Taizé, The Spiritual Disciplines, Taizé, 1968.

6 Beginnings

1 *The Wisdom of the Desert Fathers*, III, trans. Benedicta Ward, SLG, 1975. Note that an anchorite or hermit is a monk who lives alone.
2 Luke 5.8.
3 Rule of Benedict, Chapter LXXIII.
4 Rule of Benedict, Chapter LXXIII.

5 *101 Sonnets*, Don Paterson, Faber and Faber, 1999.
6 Matthew 13.51–52, Revised English Bible.
7 'East Coker' in *The Four Quartets*, T. S. Eliot, Faber and Faber 1979.